● THE LABOR UNION HANDBOOK ●

THE LABOR UNION HAND- BOOK

MURIEL MERKEL

• Beaufort Books, Inc. / New York / Toronto •

FOR MY MOTHER AND FATHER

Material excerpted from the book *Toil and Trouble* by Thomas R. Brooks. Second Edition, Copyright © 1964, 1971 by Thomas R. Brooks. Reprinted by permission of Delacorte Press.

Material excerpted from pages 20-21 of *American Labor Unions*, Second Revised Edition, by Florence Peterson. Copyright © 1963 by Harper & Row, Publishers, Inc. Reprinted courtesy of the publisher.

Material excerpted from the book *Labor* by Neil W. Chamberlain. Copyright © 1958 by The McGraw Hill Book Company, Inc. Reprinted by permission of the publisher.

Material excerpted from pages 85 and 87 of the book *Labor in the United States* by Sanford Cohen, Fifth Edition. Copyright © 1979 by Charles E. Merrill Publishing Company. Reprinted by permission of the publisher.

Material excerpted from the book *American Labor* by Henry Pelling. Copyright © 1960 by the University of Chicago. Reprinted by permission of The University of Chicago Press.

Material excerpted from *Dictionary of Industrial Relations* by Harold S. Roberts by permission of the publisher, The Bureau of National Affairs, Inc. Copyright © 1966 by BNA Incorporated.

Library of Congress Cataloging in Publication Data
Merkel, Muriel.
    The labor union handbook.
    Includes index.
    1. Trade-unions—United States. I. Title.
HD6508.M39   1982   331.88′0973   82-12831
ISBN 0-8253-0101-7

Published in the United States by Beaufort Books, Inc., New York.
Published simultaneously in Canada by General Publishing Co. Limited

Designer: Liney Li
Printed in the U.S.A.   First Edition
10   9   8   7   6   5   4   3   2   1

ACKNOWLEDGMENTS

I should like to thank the following for their assistance:

International Ladies' Garment Workers' Union, in particular, Solomon Berger, Administrative Director of the ILGWU Health Center; Henoch Mendelsund, Director of the Archives; and Jay Mazur, Vice President of the ILGWU and Manager of Local 2325.

Canadian Consulate General in New York, in particular, Mrs. Sheila Purse and her staff.

Margaret E. Sutter, for her intelligent preparation of the manuscript.

CONTENTS

Introduction   11

1   Colonial Times to the Civil War   14

2   Strife and Bloodshed   27

3   Repression and Progress (1890 to 1917)   41

4   Two World Wars   61

5   Fireworks in the Labor Movement   80

6   The "New" Unionists   97

7   Union Structure and Operations   113

8   What Union Membership Means   129

9   What Does a Union Do?   143

10   What's in a Contract?   154

11   What Is Collective Bargaining?   167

12   Strikes and Peaceful Settlement   176

13   Neighbor to the North   190

Glossary   206

Suggestions for Further Reading   218

Index   221

The Unions
in Our Lives

When less than twenty-five percent of the work force is unionized, why should the other seventy-five percent be interested in understanding labor unions? One reason is, as citizens, we vote for the representatives who make the laws affecting unions. Another is, as stockholders, some of us are part owners of companies that may be unionized, non-unionized, or hostile to unions. Still a more compelling reason is that unions are involved in our daily lives.

Do you use public transportation to go to and from your job? Your drivers, conductors, and the repair shop mechanics may be union members.

Do you have a child in school or college? The teachers, professors, administrators, and maintenance staff may be union members.

Are you a tenant or a property owner? The sanitation people may be union members.

Have you ever been hospitalized or have you ever had a family member in a hospital or health care institution? The licensed professional nurses and technicians, the administrative staff, the

11

food preparation workers, and the cleaning people may be union members.

Do you travel by bus, plane, or ship? The operating and the maintenance crews may be union members.

Do you attend the theater or concerts, watch motion pictures or television, play tapes or records, read newspapers or magazines? The artists, performers, musicians, writers, printers, and technicians may be union members.

Do you send or receive mail? Your postal workers may be union members.

You may find union members among your friends and family. Some may tell you why they are union members—through conviction or compulsion—and be able to describe how their union works and what their membership means to them. Some may be satisfied, some may be critical of the union.

Most of us, however, are conscious of unions only when our comfort, convenience, or health is threatened by union activity—a strike, for example. Our reactions tend to be more emotional than rational; we tend to disregard the issues and concentrate on our own feelings.

Ask an urban worker who has had to walk or bicycle to his job because of a transportation strike. Ask a worker who could not get to work at all and lost pay. Ask a frantic son or daughter with an aged and helpless parent in a nursing home where the staff has walked out. Ask home owners in a city where the fire fighters have struck. Ask and you will get the views you would expect.

So it is by the walkouts that exhaust, frustrate, enrage or frighten us that we learn one fact about unions: they strike. If this is all we know about unions and the collective bargaining process we know very little about the role and significance of the unions in our countries and what we may owe them. We are ignorant then of the attempts unions have made to equalize power between employer and employee; to protect workers against arbitrary, capricious, and often unfair actions by employers; and to bring about improvements in working conditions and the quality of life from which we all have benefited.

This book is a guide to the international unions in the United States and Canada and to their locals. It is neither an analysis nor a critical study but rather an overall view. Every subject touched upon can be studied in depth by those who are interested; a list of selected books is provided, and others can be found giving further insights into various aspects of the labor movement.

For the United States the laws referred to are the federal laws that affect most enterprises in interstate commerce. Those that are in intrastate commerce are subject to the labor laws of the fifty states. Information about the labor laws in a particular state can be obtained from the appropriate state agency.

The information about union policies and practices presented in this book applies to most unions, but there are exceptions. In dealing with almost two hundred different international unions, we are dealing with the rule and not the exception. What we describe is *generally, usually,* or *ordinarily* the case, not what occurs rarely or infrequently.

Finally, understanding unions does not require us to overlook or condone excesses. The purpose of this book is to facilitate understanding, to provide a factual framework showing how unions came about, to show how they operate and the attitudes of public and government toward labor organizations.

CHAPTER 1

Colonial Times to the Civil War

Understanding the labor movement in the United States requires knowledge of the country's history, from its days as a colony of Great Britain after a revolution, a civil war, and wars fought all over the globe through the period of expansion and industrialization up to the present. Also needed is understanding of the different kinds of people who immigrated here, from the first settlers to the latest wave of immigrants from the Orient.

The explorers and the traders did not put down roots here. But the settlers, for the most part, came originally with the aid and support of the English crown, which chartered companies or individuals and gave grants of land (land which had been claimed in the name of the crown and which was simply taken, in most instances, from its inhabitants, the various Indian tribes). Some of the first settlers, men of wealth, brought their servants with them. Others, like the Puritan settlers of New England, expected to work the land themselves. Some skilled craftsmen accompanied both types of settlers.

The first major problem was the shortage of skilled labor, as well as a scarcity of semi-skilled or unskilled labor. Unlike Europe, the early colonies did not have hordes of peasants or landless laborers. The skilled craftsman who worked in colonial America got high wages and, more often than not, could get land of his own and set himself up as an independent tradesman or independent farmer (or both) at a rate of rapid advancement virtually unknown in Europe or Great Britain.

America was then a rural society. In the South planters grew specialized crops, rice and tobacco, for example, for export. Their large plantations required substantial labor forces. Small-scale industry required workers. Richard B. Morris, in *The American Worker,* points out that:

> *The colonies established glass industries, brick and tile yards, and potters' kilns; bog ores proved suitable for making castings and hollow ware, and rock ores fed furnaces and forge industries. A flourishing lumber industry supplied related activities such as shipbuilding and the production of naval stores and potash. New England's white pine provided masts, yards and spars for the Royal Navy; the white oak of the Middle Colonies supplied valuable stock for the cooperage industry, and other hard woods of that area were used in the cabinetmaker's trade; in the South, yellow pine was the principal source of tar, pitch and turpentine. Fishing and whaling required substantial fleets and thousands of sailors.*

In England the government, convinced that the country was overpopulated, encouraged the poor to emigrate and allowed skilled workers to do so as well. The official attitude changed by 1765 when a law forbidding the emigration of skilled workers was passed. But, if someone else would foot the bill, the government was happy to see the poor, the homeless, and the criminal class off to the American colonies.

At this time, too, Morris states, skilled workers were coming to the American colonies from other countries: Swedes to Delaware, Walloons and Dutch to New Amsterdam, Polish workers to Virginia, among others.

Nevertheless, labor was scarce. So, the English settlers devised several forms of bound labor, one for white Europeans and another for black Africans.

White Europeans came, or were forced to come, as indentured servants. Their indenture was for a period of years—four was the usual number—either by contract or by the custom of the colony. The white immigrants, also called "redemptioners" or "freewillers," bound themselves over as servants to pay off the cost of their passage to America. Morris explains that the planters who assumed the transportation charges got headrights or land grants for each immigrant they took over. Usually, however, the business was carried on by merchants, often shipmasters, who specialized in the sale of indentures. The methods used to round up prospects would not bear close inspection. The merchants employed recruiters known as "crimps." Many men and women were brought aboard ship against their will for transportation to the colonies and were sold as bond servants. As many as half the redemptioners would die aboard ship because of lack of food, disease, or poor sanitation. Once landed, families might be broken up by sales to different masters.

England also provided another source of bound labor: convicts. People convicted of lesser crimes were transported for seven years, those convicted of serious offenses for fourteen years. Some Americans, Benjamin Franklin among them, deplored the dumping of convicts on the colonies. However, the cost of convict labor was cheap, and employers, especially in the South, continued to utilize it.

Other sources of bound labor were persons convicted in the colonies of larceny. Colonial courts generally sentenced them to corporal punishment and restitution (not death, as was common in England). If the prisoner could not make restitution, the court would have him bound out to service. If a servant ran away and was captured, the court would sentence him to as many as ten days for every day of unauthorized leave. Free workers as well as indentured servants were subject to this policy.

Lastly, debtors provided bound labor. Unlike England, with its debtors' prisons, the colonies thought it a waste of labor to imprison a debtor. Instead, he was released to work for the creditor until his debt was satisfied.

The second major source of labor for the colonies was one that almost tore the new republic apart in the middle of the nineteenth century and has continued to have reverberations down to the present day: slave labor.

The slave trade was not new: as the new American colonies, with their need for labor, grew, slave traders saw their opportunity for enrichment and took it. What resulted was known as the "triangular trade," operating between Africa, New England, and the West Indies or the southern states. New England rum, guns, gun powder, and other goods were bartered with West African chiefs who supplied the slaves. The slave ships were horrors: people were chained together with no room to stand, sit, or lie down properly. Foul food, water, and disease took many lives.

The first blacks who came to Virginia in 1619 were treated as bound servants and freed after their term of servitude ended. By 1640 the custom of life-long servitude had taken hold. The system was self-perpetuating, and southerners regarded it as essential to their economic well-being. Half a million blacks were living in America by 1775. More than three fifths of them lived in the Carolinas and Virginia. In South Carolina slaves comprised the majority of the population.

Slaves eventually replaced indentured servants in the fields. Indentured white artisans were used to train blacks in their crafts. Gradually, the whites released from their indentures moved to upland regions, most of them surviving as "poor whites."

The free laborers, especially the skilled, could fare well as wages remained high. Sometimes fringe benefits, such as food or rum, were given. And, even if buying a piece of land left them on the brink of poverty, they were land holders. European visitors to the United States in the early nineteenth century commented on the high wages and standard of living enjoyed by "mechanics," a term used to mean anyone who worked with his hands. The scarcity of labor making for high pay, the ready availability and acquisition of land, and the common cause that both worker and employer had in the revolution—the political struggle against English rule—may help to explain why the labor movement in America was not a class war.

The War for Independence halted the flow of bound labor, but only for a time. Imprisonment for debt still existed; it was not abolished until the 1830s. Slavery continued despite the opposition of many southern patriots to the institution. Five of the original thirteen states initiated programs of emancipation before 1787; two others followed not long afterward. What seemed lacking was an effective plan for the black population after emancipation. The white laboring classes were not enthusiastic about the prospect of competition from black workers, a position that continues today.

Both merchants and mechanics, however, joined in the effort to secure ratification of the new Constitution; in New York City some four thousand mechanics representing more than fifty crafts, marched to celebrate ratification. Richard. B. Morris comments in *The American Worker:*

> *Under such harmonious auspices was launched the new federal ship of state. Such unity proved short-lived, however. Labor and capital would part company along political lines by the middle of the 1790s, and a series of notable strikes in the following decade would signalize the start of a trade union movement fashioned to meet the changing conditions of labor in an emerging industrial society.*

At the end of the American Revolution the country was still a rural one. The population was less than four million; communication and transportation were difficult; industry still consisted mainly of artisans and masters; the factory system was unknown. Unions were almost nonexistent, although a few early associations would spring up from time to time for a particular purpose and then fade out.

Many workers were indentured; others were slaves. It would be impossible for them to form unions. Unions require free men, not those bound by contract or for life. Not that the bound laborers, white and black, did not rebel from time to time. They did but were put down, often ruthlessly.

A number of factors militated against permanent employee associations as we know them today. Arthur A. Sloane and Fred Witney in *Labor Relations* mention four:

1. The market for products was a local one and generally noncompetitive. Close social ties existed between worker and employer, often working in the employer's home at a relaxed pace.

2. Workers had a large measure of job security, since skilled labor was scarce. Colonial labor laws required apprenticeship training for employment in many trades and prescribed conditions for discharge.

3. Mechanics could always leave and move on—the West was opening and land was plentiful and cheap.

4. The law ratio of labor to natural resources meant that increases in the price of products lagged behind wage increases.

Some attempts at unions did develop, even in colonial times. For example in 1778 the journeymen printers of New York City combined to demand an increase in wages. The union disbanded after the increase was given. In Philadelphia in 1786 the printers struck

—the earliest authenticated strike—for a minimum wage of six dollars a week. An unsuccessful strike of Philadelphia carpenters occurred in 1791; they demanded a ten-hour day and additional pay for overtime. In 1794 the Typographical Society was organized by the New York printers; it lasted a little over ten years.

Note that these were local activities and that they were by journeymen and skilled artisans not by unskilled laborers or factory hands. Note too that no encouragement by government existed and that the developing hostile attitude of employers would soon be reflected in the courts of the new republic.

Major changes in the new country now began. First was the great expansion into the West, bringing with it the need for transportation as well as skilled workers in the new settlements. The 1807 Embargo Act and the War of 1812 turned American capital to American investments. In *Toil and Trouble* Thomas R. Brooks mentions that besides investment in domestic manufacturing, Americans were beginning what was to become a major occupation: road building. He states that a federal highway costing seven million dollars was pushed west through the Cumberland Gap, reaching Wheeling, West Virginia, in 1817. He says:

A mania for canal building spurred a network of navigable waterways in New York, Pennsylvania, Ohio, Indiana, and other states. Work on the Erie Canal commenced on July 4, 1817; on July 4, 1825, 363 miles of canal from Albany to Buffalo opened for traffic.

The development of transportation opened new markets for American retail merchants.

Early in the nineteenth century, the country was undergoing social, economic, and technological changes that would turn the United States into an industrial power. The rural nation of under four million would number thirty-one million by the Civil War, and the search for cheap labor to feed the factories would have an impact on government, employers, and labor.

Major changes in the labor movement were slower to begin. The Journeymen Cordwainers (Shoemakers) Society of Philadelphia, organized in 1794, is an example. They had organized themselves in self-defense against their masters (who themselves had organized five years earlier). They wanted a minimum wage, either a flat rate per day or for each task or piece of work completed and demanded what we would call a closed shop. They compelled masters to hire and retain only members of the society and insisted outsiders had to join the society if they wanted to work. They also turned out—struck—for their demands. Other early strikes also took place; sometimes journeymen struck even before they formed a union. Most of the strikes were over wages, but in 1806 the Philadelphia Cordwainers turned out in a strike to uphold the closed shop. The strike was not peaceful; they broke windows in demonstrations against their employers and beat up the scabs (workers who crossed their lines).

The employers resorted to legal action. They induced the public prosecutor to invoke the common law doctrine of criminal conspiracy. (Common law is a body of law based on judicial decisions, not on statutes.) In 1806, after a strike, the Philadelphia Cordwainers were tried for criminal conspiracy. The charges were that they had acted in combination to raise wages and had injured others. The union was found guilty and fined. As a result, it went bankrupt and disbanded.

Employers and merchants thus used a legal weapon from the English courts, which treated labor combinations as illegal conspiracies. Employers thought that strikes, if successful, would harm communities and that the closed shop (only union members hired or employed), was an intolerable interference with the freedom of artisans who chose not to join a society. This point of view, which the judges, attorneys, and juries agreed with at that time, still echoes today in some quarters. One must remember, too, that the employers and merchants were men of property, and in that society, so were the judges.

The doctrine of criminal conspiracy, which was applied until the middle of the nineteenth century, holds that what one individual can do legally, for example, requesting a wage increase, becomes illegal if a number of workers take the same action, as in the case of a union. The union itself thus became an illegal organization.

This doctrine prevailed in the courts until the 1842 landmark decision of Chief Justice Lemuel Shaw of Massachusetts.

In the case of *Commonwealth* v. *Hunt* the court ruled that labor unions, as such, were legal organizations and that a conspiracy must be a combination of two or more persons by some concerted action to accomplish some criminal or unlawful purpose or to accomplish some purpose not in itself criminal or unlawful by criminal or unlawful means.

The case in which this ruling was made involved Boston shoe-makers who had organized a closed shop. Chief Justice Shaw, disagreeing with the prosecutor, said a closed shop could be established for good as well as bad purposes. Shaw's reputation was such that other courts followed his lead, but the early unions still faced barriers: the doctrine of civil conspiracy and the doctrine of illegal purpose. Courts began to look into the motives for union demands.

An important difference between the doctrines of criminal conspiracy and civil conspiracy was that under criminal conspiracy the public prosecutor brought the charge against the unions; under the civil conspiracy doctrine the employer himself brought the charge. The penalty usually took the form of money damages, which most unions could ill afford.

Toward the last quarter of the nineteenth century, the labor injunction came into use. Instead of waiting for the commission of acts that damaged him and then suing for damages, the employer could petition the court for an injunction to stop the action before the union took it.

The use of the injunction not only supported the doctrine of civil conspiracy; it placed a powerful weapon in the hands of employers to be used against effective action by a union. Not until the next century and the Norris-LaGuardia Act of 1932 was any curb put upon the use of the injunction in labor disputes.

In the first half of the nineteenth century sporadic efforts were made to form unions, but most of them were local associations and few had the stamina to survive in a hostile climate. One that did was the Typographical Union, a national union founded in 1852 and still functioning today. In 1859 the Iron Molders' Union was organized in Philadelphia. It was the forerunner of the Molders' and Allied Worker's Union. Out of the Molders' Union came one of America's first labor leaders, William H. Sylvis. A self-educated man, Sylvis was one of the founders of the Molders and became its president. He was also one of the founders in 1866 of the National Labor Union, a national association of unions. (It had a short life, going out existence in 1872.) Unfortunately, Sylvis died in 1869 at the age of forty-one, before he had any real opportunity to make his mark in the labor movement.

The National Labor Union, however, was not the first attempt to bring a number of unions together. And there were a number of different trade or craft unions in existence before the 1830s despite the opposition of employers and the generally hostile judgements of the law. The country's first city central type of organization on record was organized in Philadelphia in July, 1827. It was called the Mechanics' Union of Trade Associations and was composed of the representatives of fifteen trades. Its original goal was the ten-hour day. The organization converted itself into the Workingmen's Party in 1828 but was out of existence by 1832.

At this time a number of workingmen's parties were organized. They were short-lived but their goals were important: abolition of imprisonment for debt, universal free education, abolition of child labor, a mechanics' lien law (meaning that if the employer went into bankruptcy, the claims of employees for wages were the first obligation, taking precedence over other obligations). These aims eventually became law.

Internal dissension split these workingmen's parties, and the major political parties also wooed them. Workers in the East were likely to vote on ethnic lines, the Americans and British immigrants for the Whigs, and the Germans and Irish for the Democrats. Between 1790 and 1830 about four hundred thousand immigrants entered the country, which by 1830 had thirteen million inhabitants. The first unions and the early labor movement in the United States were made up largely of native-born Americans.

Although the first city central body had disappeared in 1834 an attempt was made to establish a national labor federation. This was the National Trades' Union, founded in New York City.

By 1840 two events combined to all but wipe out the growing labor movement. In 1837 a severe economic recession began and lasted for a number of years. At the same time waves of immigrants came to America. The difficulties of union survival in a depression and the competition from immigrants who would work for low wages formed a pattern that recurs in American history.

Unions staged over four hundred strikes from 1853 to 1854, most for higher wages. The political aspirations of some of the earlier unions and movements gave way to concentration on the closed shop, rules of apprenticeship, wages and methods of pay, strike, and other benefits.

In *The American Worker* Edward Pessen writes:

These strikes did not follow negotiations as we know them. Instead, unions would decide on their objectives and then issue notices such as the following: "On Wednesday evening September 4 the Bricklayers and Plasterers by a unanimous vote declared that they would not work after Wednesday the 11th inst. for a sum less than $2.00 per day, on and after that day." If the employer accepted these terms, a "trade agreement" was concluded. Such agreements were sought not only from individual employers but from employers' associations, in order to establish uniform wages and other conditions in a craft. Strikes were often directed against recalcitrant or non-association employers.

The individual unions again attempted to organize themselves on a national scale, but the Panic of 1857 had a devastating effect. Only three of the dozen or so national unions created in the 1850s survived: the National Typographical Union, the Machinists' and Blacksmiths' International Union, and the Iron Molders' International Union.

On the eve of the Civil War the spokesmen for organized labor preferred conciliation to bloodshed. Yet once the Civil War broke out, most northern labor leaders rallied to the cause. One estimate is that mechanics and laborers constituted forty-two percent of the Union Army. Many skilled workers volunteered, decimating union ranks. One Philadelphia union closed up for the duration. Foreign-born and native workers, alike, were strongly in support of the Union, although some opposed government policies such as emancipation or a draft of the poor.

Pessen says the war had mixed consequences for labor:

Several western states passed antistrike laws and eastern states gave serious consideration to such measures. Nor did the national governmnt display much sympathy for labor. Workers in the great federal workshops in Nashville were defrauded of what they believed to be their rightful wages. They were not given the promised time and a half for overtime and were deprived of part of their wages if they quit. In the Brooklyn Navy Yard the back pay of striking molders was confiscated.

Military force was used against striking workers. Leaders in the strike at the famous Parrott gun works in Cold Spring, New York, were imprisoned without trial. General Burbridge drove strikers back to work at the point of bayonets. General Rosecrans charged picket lines and strike meetings. Soldiers in Tioga County, Pennsylvania, arrested the striking miners' leaders, forcing the rank and file to surrender to the owners under the threat of starvation.

Strikes not only persisted but also multiplied because of the perennial problem for workers, a rising cost of living not matched by wage increases for the unskilled. During the war, unions increased in number. The unions consisted mainly of urban artisans. Trades' assemblies of different unions in a city developed. Between 1861 and 1865 more than a dozen national unions emerged: miners, locomotive engineers, cigarmakers, plasterers, tailors, printers, bricklayers. Says Pessen: "Owing much to technological and commerical changes that rendered more parochial unionism obsolete, these unions arose not so much because of the Civil War as out of it."

CHAPTER 2

Strife
and
Bloodshed

During the years between America's emergence as an independent nation and the end of the Civil War, the United States had become one of the leading industrial powers. But the workers who had contributed so much enjoyed very little. The Civil War had brought them neither well-being nor wealth.

The wartime population of twenty-three million had tripled to almost eighty million. Between 1865 and 1900, twelve million people came to America from Europe. About one million were British, about half the twelve million were German and Irish. From southeastern Europe, lured by promises of work, came Italians, Croatians, Ukrainians, Hungarians, and Poles. By 1890 the German and Irish immigrants were outnumbered by the others. The factory system was developing rapidly. The small businessman was finding his existence difficult; the men with money and power were pooling resources in trusts and corporations.

Unions had a high casualty rate between 1861 and 1871. With the war and the participation in it, union membership had dwindled. Very few of these unions survived until the establishment of the American Federation of Labor in 1886. Yet, just before the war, city-wide trades' assemblies had arisen, evidencing a need for associations to further union causes and to provide mutual support. This need for association produced the International Industrial Assembly of North America in 1864. It met only once, but it produced one significant achievement: a constitutional provision for a strike fund to be financed by a per capita tax.

In 1866 the nation suffered another depression, and again attention turned to reform, in particular the idea of an eight-hour work day, which, in turn, stimulated the notion of a national labor federation. By then a resurgence of trade unions had begun (between 1864 and 1874, a number of new national unions were organized, including the present-day Brotherhood of Locomotive Engineers).

In 1866 in Baltimore a convention of delegates from local trade unions, city trades' assemblies, national trade unions, and the eight-hour leagues formed the National Labor Union. In later years it included delegates from farmers' associations, black groups, the Women's Suffrage Association, and other reform movements. The National Labor Union was a loose federation. With representatives from so many different groups, it was torn by dissension and could not decide whether it was a trade union organization or a legislative reform group. It drifted into social reform, lost the support of craftsmen, and went out of existence in 1872. Its main efforts had been in behalf of the greenback movement and the eight-hour day. The eight-hour day is a recurring theme in reform and union movements of the time. Actually, the first federal eight-hour day was passed by Congress in 1868; it applied only to laborers, workmen, and mechanics employed by or on behalf of the United States Government. Several states also passed eight-hour laws, but workers were forced to sign agreements for longer hours. (The laws had no enforcement provisions.)

The years after the Civil War continued the pattern of prosperity followed by depression, of growing industrialization and immigration, and the rise and fall of trade unions. What was also becoming apparent was hostility and violence between employer and employee to a degree unparalleled before these years of expansion.

In *The Practice of Unionism,* Jack Barbash comments that no political democracy offered unions a more hostile environment than did the United States and that this hostility gave American unionism a character different from any other labor movement.

"Aggressive industrial capitalism" is the term used by Sanford Cohen,* who points out that another important factor favoring the industrialists was a sympathetic congress and judiciary.

The employers could and did use labor spies, strikebreakers, lockouts, blacklists, injunctions, and yellow dog contracts (see glossary). They also often had use of the state militia and federal troops. The unions had the strike and the boycott. No laws either encouraged, protected, or controlled collective bargaining between employer and unions. Yet the union movement, despite setbacks, put down roots and grew.

In reaction to all-out attacks by employers, labor groups also resorted to violence. Probably the most violent group was the Molly Maguires, a secret group in the anthracite coal fields that made its appearance in the 1850s but which was most active in the 1860s and 1870s.

They were not a labor union or organization, but a group of individuals, an offshoot of the Ancient Order of Hibernians, who had used terrorist tactics against the landlords in Ireland, and used those tactics in the United States to harass mine owners and their agents. They wrecked trains, blew up mines, sniped at and murdered employers and their managers who would not cooperate with them, and ran strike breakers out of the mine fields.

*Cohen, Sanford: *Labor in the United States.* (Columbus, Ohio: Charles E. Merrill Publishing Co., 1979) p. 96.

Enter Alan Pinkerton, a former spy for the North during the Civil War. The mine operators hired him to attempt to break the Molly Maguires. He used one of his operatives to infiltrate the Molly Maguires under an assumed name. Like other *agents provacateurs*, he was quite successful. He became secretary of his district, urged his men on to more acts of violence, and gathered evidence needed to destroy the group.

In 1876, ten of the Molly Maguires were hanged and fourteen were jailed, largely on the strength of the agent's unsupported testimony.

Pinkerton became a hated name in the labor movement. The agency made a reputation for supplying strikebreakers and labor spies. A popular song of the era was "Daddy Was Killed by the Pinkerton Men."

Another organization, the Knights of St. Crispin, appears to have been organized, secretly, in Milwaukee in 1867, mainly in reaction to the introduction of new machinery, which threatened the shoemakers' customary methods of work. (St. Crispin is the patron saint of shoemakers.) After the Civil War shoemakers were hard hit by the employers' use of machinery that would bring the factory system of specialized operations into shoemaking, thus reducing or eliminating the need for the craftsmen. The new machinery would enable employers to hire "green hands" and the Crispins protested. By 1870 they were the largest national union, with a membership of fifty thousand, and had run several successful strikes. In the end, however, the new machinery defeated them (as new machinery was to do to other traditional crafts), and the employers were able to break the union. The Panic of 1873 spelled the end of this union.

The Panic of 1873 set the stage for a virtual warfare between capital and labor that has persisted, although to a much lesser extent, down to our own day. Not that every strike or organizing drive is accompanied by premeditated violence on either or both sides; not that federal and state laws do not now provide orderly methods for resolving differences; not that most unions do not negotiate at the bargaining table; not that most employers do not use lawyers and labor specialists rather than goon squads—but planned violence has continued, as witness the California grape industry in the 1960s.

Without going into every instance of nineteenth century industrial violence, two examples can be seen: the Tompkins Square Riot and the Railroad Riots. The background is described by Sanford Cohen in *Labor in the United States:*

> *The depression that began in 1873 and lasted until 1879 provided the setting for the labor uprisings. The economic upheaval that accompanied the Civil War foreshadowed a difficult process of post-war readjustment. . . .*
>
> *The depression was severe. This was due partly to the overly rapid railroad expansion. Too much of the mileage, according to one observer, connected nothing in particular. Since railroad construction accounted for such a substantial part of the total investment activity at this time, the depressing effect of curtailment in railroad expansion extended far beyond this industry. The price level dropped sharply and business failures were common. Confusion in the government's monetary policy also contributed to the severity of the depression.*
>
> *For the workers, all of this meant unemployment, hunger, and despair. Those who continued to work saw their wages slashed mercilessly. As the effects of the panic spread, thousands of the unemployed gathered in mass meetings to protest the pitiful conditions of their lives. With tension mounting, only a spark was necessary to touch off a social explosion. Unfortunately, more than one spark was provided.*

At this time the socialists were active in the various unemployment demonstrations. In *Toil and Trouble* Thomas R. Brooks mentions that thousands of workers, at "the behest of socialist-organized Committee of Public Safety," marched into Tompkins Square in New York City on January 13, 1874. Mounted police, hearing that radicals were to speak, charged into the crowd wielding their clubs. Hundreds were injured. No one, however, was killed. That distinction remains for the Railroad Riots of 1877, which Brooks calls "the first great clash between capital and labor." Although the railroads continued, even after the Panic, to pay dividends of eight and ten percent, they cut wages.

Hours of work were long, pay was often in arrears, and trackmen on the Erie Railroad lived as squatters on land owned by the railroad. They were suddenly ordered to pay rent or get out. Some other railroads took back the passes their men used to go back and forth from work. The engineers on another railroad were ordered to quit their union, the Brotherhood of Locomotive Engineers. The engineers planned a strike, but spies, mainly Pinkerton men, thwarted their plans.

In 1877 the Pennsylvania Railroad announced a ten percent wage cut. A secret Trainmen's Union, a kind of industrial union, taking in shop men, conductors, engineers, trackmen, and brakemen, was organized. The union grew, and planned a strike but collapsed because of internal conflicts.

Then the Baltimore and Ohio announced a ten-percent wage cut. On July 16, 1877, the day the new wage rate was to go into effect, a series of protest strikes erupted. At Martinsburg, West Virginia, the militia was called out by the governor at the request of a Baltimore and Ohio vice president, but the military men soon fraternized with the strikers. Federal troops were requested. Disturbances broke out in every railroad center, on every railroad. In Baltimore a three-day riot ended with thirteen killed and many wounded (the National Guard and federal troops had been called in). Pittsburgh suffered an enormous amount of strife; where, as at other rail centers, the local population, including farmers, sided with the strikers.

In Pittsburgh, the militia from Philadelphia (the locals were not called out) fired into a crowd and killed twenty people. The troops had retreated to a railroad roundhouse and had to shoot their way out, killing and wounding more people as they went. A fire broke out in the freight cars at the depot; the mob looted. Order was restored by volunteer bands of citizens. Some five million dollars worth of railroad property was destroyed.

The riots were spontaneous and without direction. Cohen comments:

If they had better direction, it is possible they would have been less easily quelled and, at least to a small degree, more successful. As it was, mobs of workers turned out to be a poor match against armed troops, hostile government officials, and an inflamed public opnion. The driving capitalistic spirit that motivated the railroad officialdom had no room for accomodation of deeply felt grievances of workers. The inflexibility of employers—the president of the New York Central refused even to admit that his workers were on strike—their callous disregard of economic poverty, and the inability of the labor organizations to channel the discontent into effective protest created a situation where violence was the most probable result.

Brooks puts it succinctly: ''The relationship of labor to capital was irretrievably changed. The old master-journeyman relationship was forever buried with the ashes of the Pittsburgh roundhouse.''

The upheavals on the railroads did not squelch unionism. Just one year after the Railroad Riots the Noble Order of the Knights of Labor began organizing openly and held its first national general assembly.

Like the Knights of St. Crispin, the Knights of Labor started as a secret society in Philadelphia in 1869. The Knights evolved out of an old Association of Garment Cutters which was dissolved in 1869. Some former Garment Cutters organized the Knights because they felt the need for association. This secrecy served a practical purpose: the less employers knew about a struggling labor organization, the better.

The leader of the Knights of Labor was a garment cutter and former Baptist minister named Uriah Stephens. The Knights maintained secrecy until 1878, when they openly began organizing both skilled and unskilled workers. At the height of its power, in 1886, the Knights had about seven hundred thousand members. But as the American Federation of Labor emerged, the Knights declined.

An example of organization by the Knights is seen in the story of a young worker named Harry Skeffington who became a Knight of Labor on his eighteenth birthday. In *The American Worker,* David Montgomery tells how not long afterward, he was elected Master Workman of Local Assembly 64 in Philadelphia. In 1881 Harry was ordered to organize the city's largest shoe firm, John Mundell and Co.

Harry got a job in the sole-cutting room. Soon, he discovered the workers' main grievance: after each seasonal layoff the old hands were rehired, but with the news that they would have to take a "temporary" wage cut. Since they needed jobs they accepted the condition. Then, after several months, the older and higher piece rate would be restored, just before another layoff. Harry persuaded the workers to join the union and convinced them to reject any wage cut at the beginning of the next season.

The company, surprised by this move, restored full pay to the cutters but tried to compensate by cutting the wages of the women who marked or stitched shoe parts. One of the women, Mary Sterling, jumped onto her work bench and called upon the other women to walk out. Off they marched. Harry then called out the men. The cutters marched out, along with other men in the company.

For several weeks, none of Mundell's seven hundred employees came to work. The women formed a local assembly of their own (the Knights did not admit women officially). Along with picket duty the women ran fund-raising bazaars and concerts at the assembly hall. Soon other employers urged Mundell to settle; their own workers were going to the strike festivities instead of to their jobs. Mundell settled, and the Knights became a power in Philadelphia's shoe industry. Mary Sterling went to the Knights General Assembly and persuaded them to open their doors to women.

By 1884 the Knights had eleven local assemblies in Philadelphia, each representing different crafts or groups of occupations. They formulated work rules and wage demands. Within each factory a shop union, elected by the workers, handled grievances and enforced the rules of the local assemblies. To keep track of the numerous piece rates in the shoe industry, each plant had one male and one female statistician. Grievances that the shop committee could not resolve went to a city-wide arbitration committee composed of seven Knights and seven employers.

Feeling their power, however, workers steadily increased their demands and struck frequently. By 1887 the infuriated employers, the Shoe Manufacturers' Association, responded to a walkout by one hundred sixty handsewing benchmen by firing all employees. They refused to take any of them back unless they repudiated the Knights of Labor. The workers held out for a month or so and then, craft by craft, drifted back to work.

The story of the rise and fall of organized workers in the Philadelphia shoe industry was duplicated in one industry after another during the last decades of the nineteenth century. Unionism achieved its greatest strength among coopers (those who made or repaired wooden casks) and anthracite coal miners in the early 1870s; among longshoremen, packinghouse workers, iron and steel workers, and bituminous miners in the mid-1880s; and among iron molders, railroad men, and building tradesmen in the early 1890s. The Knights of Labor owed its growth to the depression of 1873, to the influx of coal miners, and to the strikes and upheavals of 1877. Secrecy was, in the beginning, a practical matter, since the infiltration of labor spies could result in the death of a union. But Stephens, the leader of the Knights was a Mason, and the secret rituals of the Masons provided similar rituals for the Knights.

By 1878 the Knights came out into the open. At this, their first general assembly, they adopted a constitution and named Stephens Grand Master Workman. A significant innovation of this assembly was institution of a per capita tax on all members, to be paid to a general executive.

By this time secrecy had ceased to be an advantage. Because of the Molly Maguires, secrecy was associated with criminal activity. Moreover, many Knights were Catholic, and the Church disapproved of secret societies and disliked certain quasi-religious elements in the rituals. The Knights made some concessions to the various objections, but Stephens disapproved of them and resigned. He was succeeded by Terence V. Powderly.

The Knights grew and emerged in the early 1880s as the most powerful body of workers in the country. By 1885 they had about one hundred ten thousand members; they had numbered less than twenty thousand in 1881. By 1886 they had seven hundred thousand members, mainly because of successful strikes on the railroads and the revival of interest in the eight-hour day.

Yet the Knights generally disliked strikes and preferred the boycott, a weapon brought over from Ireland. In the early 1880s because Captain Charles Boycott, an agent for landlords, had been unusually severe with tenants, no one would work his land, work for him personally, or supply him with goods. In America the boycott became a method of exerting pressure on an employer by refusing to buy his goods or services.

Although the Knights eschewed strikes and sanctioned them only when members were victimized or employers refused to arbitrate, those two categories provided sufficient room for hundreds of strikes to be called.

The Knights welcomed everyone: wage earners, professional men, farmers, and small businessmen. (It excluded bankers, stockbrokers, lawyers, doctors, professional gamblers, and those deriving their living from the manufacture or sale of intoxicating liquor.) It was one big union; not until the rise of the Congress of Industrial Organizations in the 1930s would anything like it be seen again. However, these diverse groups had different interests that could not be reconciled easily. In the West the mixed assemblies of farmers, small businessmen, and workers were different from the craftsmen of the assemblies in the East. Although Powderly was a compelling speaker, he was not sufficiently powerful as a personality to impose consistency on the Knights. He also had to make a living. His title as Grand Master Workman did not bring with it commensurate pay. So his energy and effort had to be divided, on the one hand to lead the Knights and on the other to provide for himself.

Sanford Cohen, *Labor in the United States,* sees the immediate causes for the dissolution of the Knights as a series of unsuccessful strikes as well as inept leadership and increasing resistance of employers. Cohen says the technological structure with the general assembly supposedly having complete authority over the districts and locals was inconsistent with the weak leadership of the group. The leadership bumbled; the locals took the initiative and often created situations with which the general assembly could not cope. They avoided conflict and violence and did not want to clash with employers. Despite this reluctance, they were unable to develop a capacity for settling disputes peacefully.

The Knights could not accommodate both the skilled and the unskilled in the organization. The skilled felt threatened by the hordes of the unskilled. Conflicts between the trades and the Knights increased; relations between Powderly and Samuel Gompers, who represented the trades union viewpoint, were bitter. Gomper had no doubts about which cause he supported. His philosophy, on behalf of trades unions, was expressed simply: more.

The history of labor unions, like any other history, does not fit neatly into compartments. While one movement is starting, flourishing or waning, others are going on at the same time. While the Knights of Labor were rising and declining, another movement, which would become dominant for many years, was in its initial stages and its origins are entwined with another bloody event—the Haymarket Square explosion.

The rival movement to the Knights of Labor was the Federation of Organized Trades and Labor Unions. In the late 1870s, after the Railroad Riots, many national unions began to revive and some new ones were started. Initially, they were not hostile to the Knights of Labor but regarded that group as unsuited to their purposes. The Knights, with their mixed assemblies, ran counter to the interests of the trades. In November 1881 the other groups held their own convention in Pittsburgh and set up the Federation of Organized Trades and Labor Unions of the United States and Canada. Their platform contained the usual union demands but stressed the necessity for legislation to protect trade-union property, as in Great Britain.

The Federation grew slowly; some of its strikes were failures. Swedish strikebreakers were used to defeat a strike of the Fall River Cotton Spinners. The Ohio Miners were defeated, too; armed Pinkertons were used to protect Swedes, Poles, Italians, and Hungarians who were brought in to work the mines.

The eight-hour day, however, was an issue that could bring together all labor groups, and it became a rallying point for socialists and anarchists as well. The Federation had called for a general strike on May 1, 1886, to promote the eight-hour day. Powderly opposed participation of the Knights in the strike, but thousands of workers went on strike on May 1, including many Knights.

Two days after the strike, in Chicago, which had been the center of action and where about eighty thousand workers struck, the police killed four strikers at the McCormick Harvester plant. A protest meeting was called for May 4 by an anarchist group. The meeting was peaceful (the mayor had given permission to hold it and was himself an observer). Shortly after the mayor left, a police inspector with a reputation for brutality marched into Haymarket Square with one hundred eighty police. He ordered the crowd to disperse. Suddenly, a bomb exploded in the ranks of the police; seven died later as a result of injuries. The police lost control and fired directly into the crowd, killing several workers and injuring many others.

The identity of the bomb thrower was never established. The whole country reacted with hysteria as well as outrage. Eight anarchists were arrested. There is agreement that no conclusive evidence of their guilt existed, yet seven were sentenced to death. Two received clemency and drew life sentences. One committed suicide. Four were hanged. An eighth was sentenced to a fifteen-year prison term. The three men in prison later were pardoned by Governor John P. Altgeld, who was attacked bitterly for his action.

The incident caused a revulsion of feeling against unions and damaged the Knights, although Powderly tried to disassociate his group from the affair. Powderly refused to join in any public appeal for clemency lest he associate the Knights with violence and anarchy. The public did not make the distinction, and anti-labor feelings were aroused by the Haymarket Explosion.

The newly established American Federation of Labor, however, did beg clemency for the convicted men, although it too condemned violence. And the Chicago Knights, also condemning violence, did plead for mercy for the men.

In 1886, which proved unpropitious for labor in general, the American Federation of Labor was established out of the Federation of Organized Trades and Labor Unions. Its early years and

growth coincided with the great explosion of industry into the
twentieth century; before the first half of that century ended,
enormous changes occurred in the relations of employers and
unions, and in the relationship of government to both capital and
labor.

CHAPTER 3

Repression and Progress (1890 to 1917)

It has been said that the Gay Nineties were not so gay for the average working person, even though some workers—about fifteen percent—did enjoy a measure of prosperity. Among the more fortunate were locomotive engineers, iron rollers, glass blowers and other skilled craftsmen who could earn from eight to eleven hundred dollars a year. David Montgomery in *The American Worker* notes that about forty-five percent of workers, the largest group, had incomes that in good times were just above the poverty level: "Molders, carpenters, machinists, mule spinners, and coal miners might manage a house or flat of four to five rooms (more, if they took in boarders) and put plenty of cheaper meat, potatoes, bread, and vegetables on the table, if the mother managed the budget skillfully and the father avoided illness or injury."

However, about forty percent of working class families lived below the poverty level. Families were crowded into a couple of rooms in tenement buildings and depended heavily on the earnings of the children: "About one fourth lived in total destitution. Many found their living by scavenging, begging, and hustling." Montgomery points out that for the children "the hallmarks of their youth were not hills, springs, and oak groves, but taverns, meeting halls, market buildings, and roundhouses. Most workers lived close by countless chimneys which belched black smoke into the air. Their children swam in polluted rivers and ponds. Ironically, pollution in smaller factory towns was often worse than the notorious filth of New York and Chicago, because raw sewage was dumped directly into the local river, and barge canals made convenient trash dumps."

Two major depressions added to the misery. One, in 1873, lasted five years. The second was in the period from 1893 to 1897. Unemployment surpassed sixteen percent of the work force. Private charities supplied bread, soup, and old clothing. For some, there was the poorhouse.

Even for those who still had jobs, depressions meant wage cuts and shorter work time. During the depression miners in the Pennsylvania anthracite coal fields averaged no more than one hundred seventy-eight work days a year. They hunted, grew their own vegetables, and survived. The more fortunate members of society —the middle and upper classes—blamed the sufferings of the unemployed and the poverty-stricken on their immorality, indolence, and ignorance. Self-made men believed that effort could carry one up the ladder of success and that anyone who really wanted work could find it. The literature of the time pictured workers in unflattering terms, as dullards or drunkards. Labor leaders were labeled "agitators" and pictured as having "sly and furtive" eyes.

However, in small industrial towns the local shopkeepers and professional men often sided with workers against the leading industrialists or corporations. One characteristic of industry in the last decades of the nineteenth century was the growth of giant corporations, the trusts (combinations of firms or corporations) and the monopolies in iron and steel, oil, coal and the railroads, for example. Ironically, the Sherman Antitrust Act, passed in 1890, which seemed to be directed against industrial monopolies and trusts, was used against labor unions. The Danbury Hatters case is one example.

The end of the nineteenth and the beginning of the twentieth century also saw rapid growth in technology. New inventions led to new industries, inventions, or improvements on earlier ones such as the incandescent light bulb, the telephone, the typewriter, the adding machine, the airplane, the phonograph, the motion picture, the automobile, all of them forerunners of the everyday equipment or machines we now take for granted.

Despite active opposition by employers, who often banded together in associations, the union movement grew. By 1904 union membership amounted to over two million, up from about four hundred fifty thousand in 1897. The number of locals affiliated with the American Federation of Labor grew from fifty-eight to one hundred twenty.

The survival of the AFL after the Haymarket Riot is worth noting, especially in view of employer opposition and public revulsion at the violence. However, the employers were focusing their attention elsewhere, bent on crushing the remnants of the Knights of Labor, while the AFL went quietly about its business. But the AFL was weak in the western part of America, leaving a vacuum which would be filled for a time by the more radical Industrial Workers of the World, nicknamed the Wobblies.

Samuel Gompers, who was president of the AFL (with the exception of 1895) from its beginning to his death in 1924, not only attempted to organize workers but to give the union movement status and respectibility. He hoped to make industrialists see the light, to accept the view that a responsible trade union movement was an asset to an industrial enterprise rather than a liability. The AFL represented a conservative type of unionism but was regarded in decidedly different ways. The employer saw it as a threat to his property and his right to conduct his business as he saw fit. The radical viewed it as a betrayal of the historical revolutionary mission of the laboring class.

It was an uphill task, then, since employer opposition was

consolidating and would, in some cases, amount to warfare against workers with the assistance of hired guns and sometimes of state and federal government forces. The size and power of the business enterprises that were in virtual control of certain industries are described by Henry Pelling in *American Labor:*

> *These enterprises were so vast that they overshadowed many of the constitutional forms of government. They had such great economic power, for good or ill, that they could influence or even control state legislatures and could also carry great weight with Congress itself. They often encountered community opposition, especially in the more egalitarian West, but to counteract it they were prepared to supply their own private police, often obtained from the Pinkerton Agency, which specialized in this type of work. When Congress attempted to prevent the monopolies from growing too strong, notably by the Interstate Commerce Act of 1887 and the Sherman Antitrust Act of 1890, their lawyers were able to find ways to avoid the more stringent provisions of the enactments, and the process of concentration went on much as before.*

Pelling adds that few effective measures were taken to insure the safety and health of the industrial workers. Industrial legislation in this country lagged far behind that of major European countries. Basic principles of workers' compensation, for example, were developed in Europe in the 1880s; similar legislation here was not initiated until about thirty years later. In 1911 New Jersey was the first state to initiate workmen's compensation. Factory inspection laws did not exist in most states and, where they did, the inspection system was often inadequate (as the Triangle Fire proved). The toll of industrial accidents, in death and in disabling injuries, was enormous. Child labor was commonplace, restricted only by the laws on school attendance, which were not always enforced.

Yet some hopeful signs were on the horizon. The managements of some large corporations began to be concerned about on-the-job safety. Some established safety committees. Others pooled information about accident causes and provided advice (U.S. Steel, for instance). In 1916 the National Council for Industrial Safety was formed.

The states began to enact laws regulating child labor. (A federal child labor law, passed in 1916, was declared unconstitutional in 1918. Another, passed in 1919, was declared unconsitutional in 1922. A proposed child labor amendment to the Constitution failed to be ratified.)

These various forms of legislation owe much to the Progressive movement of the time as well as to the efforts of reform groups.

On the eve of World War I, America had a growing population —in 1920 it reached 106.5 million—an increasing flow of immigrants (between 1903 and 1914 more than 800,000 entered every year, with a peak of 1,387,000 in 1913), and a labor movement that truly had put down roots. It was also the richest country in the world.

Given this mix of the concentration of industrial power and wealth in the hands of a few, the aspirations of workers, particularly those in unions, and the prosperity and progress of the nation, what was the attitude of government? There could be no one attitude in the United States. The executive, legislative, and judicial branches of government at the federal, state, and local levels all can have different views on labor.

From the 1890s to the 1920s, the most antagonistic attitudes were those of the courts. In the federal government the executive and legislative branches were inching toward a more sympathetic attitude. During the 1894 Pullman strike President Grover Cleveland sent in federal troops to defeat the walkout, but in 1902 President Theodore Roosevelt used the prestige of his office to force the coal operators to submit their dispute with the United Mine Workers to arbitration.

Bloody conflicts between employers and unions were characteristic of labor relations in the last decade of the nineteenth century,
and these battles continued into the twentieth. Although clashes
between management and labor even now may be marked by
violence, nothing quite like the Homestead, Pullman, Ludlow, or
Republic Steel clashes, where bullets and bayonets were freely
used by troops, hired thugs, and police, is common today.

The most famous of the nineteenth century battles took place at
Andrew Carnegie's Homestead Works on the banks of the Monon-
gahela River, near Pittsburgh. Carnegie and the union, the Amalgamated Association of Iron and Steel Workers, did not have a
hostile relationship, but when Henry Clay Frick, who was known
to be anti-union, took over as operating head, the relationship
changed.

In February 1892 the company, although engaged in negotiations with the union, announced a wage cut and then locked out its
workers two days before the existing agreement was to expire on
June 30.

All approaches to the town and the works were watched to prevent the entry of strikebreakers. But Frick had been busy before the
lockout and had contracted for the Pinkerton agency to supply three
hundred armed men. In *Toil and Trouble* Thomas R. Brooks gives
a vivid accounting of the night of July 5 when barges transporting
the Pinkerton men were towed up the river. The waiting crowd
attempted to keep the guards from disembarking at dawn. Then a
shot was fired. This provided the Pinkertons with an excuse; they
let loose a volley into the crowd. The women and children fled for
safety; the men returned the fire. Late that afternoon, the Pinkertons
on the barges surrendered. The tally: three Pinkertons and seven
workers dead and scores wounded. The Pinkertons were sent back.

About a week later, yielding to company presure, the governor
of Pennsylvania, Robert E. Pattison, sent in state militia to take
over the town. Other steel workers walked out in sympathy. The
company took legal action against the leaders at Homestead, secur-
ing indictments for murder, riot, and conspiracy.

Although the union men were vindicated in the courts, the union cause was lost. By November of 1892 the remnants of the union voted to lift the ban against working for Carnegie. The power of the union in the steel industry was crushed. Indeed, no union was to be successful in that industry until 1937 and the Steelworkers Organizing Committee of the Congress of Industrial Organizations.

Another instance where a union took on an industry giant and met defeat occurred in the railroad industry; it involved the Pullman Palace Car Company and Eugene V. Debs.

The Brotherhood of Locomotive Firemen and Engineers had been organized in 1873, the Brotherhood of Railroad Trainmen in 1883, and the Brotherhood of Maintenance of Way Employees in 1887. The various brotherhoods, however, were not affiliated with the AFL. (The Engineers are still independent.) The railroad unions had exclusionary attitudes; they organized the crafts, not the unskilled. Consequently, rivalries existed between the brotherhoods and the unorganized workers on the railroads. This friction weakened them at an especially critical time, when the companies banded together into a General Managers Association.

A strike on the Burlington railroad in 1888 failed; one result was a movement for federation of the brotherhoods, but nothing came of it. However, the former secretary-treasurer of the Locomotive Firemen, Eugene V. Debs, quit his post and tried to build a different kind of railroad union, one that would include all workers, an industrial union. The American Railway Union, which Debs organized in 1893, sought to replace the brotherhoods and to bring in all who worked for the railroads. For a while the American Railway Union enjoyed success; in a year it had one hundred fifty thousand members. It ran a successful strike against the Great Northern early in 1894. Then came George M. Pullman.

Pullman, whose company built and repaired the "palaces" on wheels, had set up a model town near Chicago for his employees. They paid eighteen dollars a month for rent. They could, of course, live elsewhere, but those who lived in Pullman were the first hired and the last fired. Brooks reports that Chicago supplied the water, at four cents a thousand gallons, to Pullman; the company charged its workers ten cents a thousand. Gas cost Pullman thirty-three cents a thousand feet, but workers paid Pullman two dollars and twenty-five cents a thousand.

During the 1893 depression Pullman raised its dividends and slashed wages twenty-five to forty percent. (Wages ranged from four to sixteen cents an hour.) But Pullman did not reduce the cost of living in the "model" town.

During the winter of 1894 Pullman workers started to join the American Railway Union. They formed a grievance committee and presented to the company their demand for restoration of the wage cuts. Pullman met with the committee and assured it that no one on it would be fired or discriminated against; a day later, three were fired. The next day three thousand walked out, demanding reinstatement of the men and a return to the former wage scale.

Debs ordered a boycott against all trains carrying Pullman cars; the strike spread. By the end of June "Debs' Rebellion" had tied up the railroads, and the General Managers Association set out to destroy the union. By hitching Pullman cars to trains that had never carried them but which did carry the mail, they provided the federal government with the basis for intervening.

President Grover Cleveland's Attorney General was Richard P. Olney, a former lawyer for the railroads. Over the protest of Governor John C. Altgeld, the president sent in federal troops who, as Altgeld and Debs feared, stirred up violence. *Agents provocateurs* of the railroads mingled with the strikers. On July 7, soldiers fired into a crowd gathered to protest the movement of a wrecking train by troops; thirty people were killed.

What really broke the strike, however, was an injunction restraining the strikers from interfering with the mails or with interstate commerce. The injunction was so broad that any action the strikers took would have placed them in contempt of court. Debs and other strike leaders were sentenced to prison for violating the injunction.

Henry Pelling in *American Labor* cites four main factors in the failure of the Pullman strike and the demise of the American Railway Union:

1. In the depression year of 1894, with a high unemployment rate, it was not difficult to find replacements for the strikers.

2. The railroad brotherhoods were hostile to the new union which, after all, was intended to supplant them. They did nothing to discourage their members from taking jobs vacated by strikers.

3. The companies cooperated closely with each other.

4. The federal government moved in quickly with injunctions and sent in troops.

Where was Gompers at this time? Although he may not have been unsympathetic, he resisted Debs' pleas for sympathy strikes. In a way the AFL was penalized for its inaction: it was later forced to spend time and effort in legal battles, many over the injunction power of the courts, a power it might have been able to counter earlier, in the Pullman case.

The new century ushered in still more labor upheaval in the United States; the conflict would rage for another thirty-five years but with a difference. Government attitudes would gradually change. President Cleveland called out the troops to quell a strike, but President Theodore Roosevelt used persuasion on both parties. Woodrow Wilson became the first American president ever to address a union convention (the AFL in Buffalo, 1917). Public attitudes, particularly toward big business, would change, especially during the Great Depression.

Hopeful signs appeared. New unions were chartered. In 1900 the AFL chartered the International Ladies' Garment Workers Union, which, at its inception, gave no hint of the strength to be exerted by an organization composed mainly of Jewish immigrants in the needle trades. The International Ladies' Garment Workers Union broke ground through collective bargaining (see chapter XI), for a wide range of social benefits such as health care and pensions that today are taken for granted by both organized and unorganized labor.

Amid the hopeful signs the particularly bitter clashes between employers and unions persisted. In 1901 the Iron, Steel, and Tin Workers (AFL) suffered another setback: It lost a strike against the newly formed United States Steel Corporation and, as a result, lost contracts at fourteen mills, and lost strength steadily thereafter.

The puddlers, who were dissatisfied with the inclusion of all steel workers in one union, left and formed the Sons of Vulcan in 1907. The American Sheet and Tin Plate Company posted a notice that after June 30, 1909, all its plants would be "open shops" (open to non-union workers). The Iron and Steel Workers struck, but had to give up after fourteen months.

The employers' answer to a bona fide labor organization was the inside or company union. These company unions were company-dominated, that is formed, financed, assisted, and dominated by employers. As on the Great Lakes, where U.S. Steel operated fleets of iron ore vessels, these inside unions denied access to the shops to delegates from labor organizations. Later, under the National Labor Relations Act, company-dominated unions became illegal, in violation of the provision barring employer support or domination of labor organizations.

The exclusion of union members from jobs (blacklisting) led to considerable violence between 1908 to 1911. Members of the International Association of Bridge and Structural Workers found they were barred from jobs by an employers' group, the National Erectors' Association. The union reacted by dynamiting non-union jobs. (They set off about seventy explosions in three years.) When, in 1910, *The Los Angeles Times* building was dynamited and twenty died, union terrorists were blamed. Detective William Burns was hired by the National Erectors' Association; he accused the union's secretary-treasurer, John H. McNamara, and his brother, James. The case became a cause célèbre, when the famous lawyer, Clarence Darrow was retained as defense counsel. The McNamara brothers pleaded guilty and drew a prison sentence; other union leaders were convicted of conspiracy, and the cause of labor received another setback.

A different chain of events occurred in the coal industry. In 1900 the United Mine Workers of America (organized in 1890) called its first strike in the Pennsylvania anthracite fields. The strike lasted a little over a month and ended in a union victory. The strike also was notable for lack of violence.

But in May 1902 the union commenced a strike that was violent. Philip Taft says in *The American Worker*:

> *Shootings, killings, and attacks upon the colliers were frequent. In the midst of the strike, George F. Baer, head of the Reading Railroad and spokesman for the mine operators penned his famous "divine right" letters. When a Wilkes-Barre photographer appealed to him on the basis of Christian principles to settle the strike, Baer replied:*
>
> *"I do not know who you are. I see that you are a Christian man; but you are evidently biased in favor of the right of the working man to control a business in which he has no interest other than to secure fair wages for the work he does. I beg of you not to be discouraged. The right and interest of the laboring man will be protected and cared for—not by the labor agitators, but by the Christian men to whom God in his infinite wisdom has given the control of the property interests of the country, and upon the successful management of which so much depends."*

President Theodore Roosevelt, who apparently did not think Providence, in its "infinite wisdom," agreed with Baer, could not get the operators to arbitrate. But an appeal to the financier J.P.

Morgan ended with the operators agreeing to a presidential arbitration commission. The union was eager to get a union man on the panel. Taft says President Roosevelt "sneaked" E. E. Clark, Grand Chief of the Order of Conductors, on the commision as an "eminent sociologist."

The presidential commision did not grant the union all it wanted. It did not recommend recognition of the union, but it did grant a ten percent wage increase, a reduction in hours of work, and the right of the miners to elect their own check weighmen and check docking bosses. The use of private guards was held to be against the public interest. On the issue of child labor, the employment of boys as breakers was deplored, and the commission said the statutory age of employment was not high enough. During the three-year life of the agreement all disputes were to go to a board of conciliation, representing operators and miners. If the board failed to resolve the dispute, an arbitrator was to be appointed by the courts.

The United Mine Workers struck the bituminous coal fields in 1919. A month later they agreed to arbitration by a commission appointed by President Wilson, which granted a wage increase but turned down the request for a six-hour day and five-day week.

In 1913 the United Mine Workers became embroiled in a clash with the Colorado Fuel and Iron Company, which was controlled by John D. Rockefeller, the founder of the family fortune. For sheer brutality, this conflict has few equals. It led to an investigation and report by a presidential commission which was hostile to the corporations and favorable to labor. It also led to the Rockefeller or Colorado Plan, which served as a model for many variations of the company union and is the basis for "corporate welfarism," or paternalism, where the company considers itself the "father" of its employees and provides such items as pensions, profit sharing, health and recreational facilities for its well-behaved "children." These programs were intended to keep employees out of unions and keep them dependent upon the company.

The United Mine Workers had been trying, unsuccessfully, to

organize the Colorado fields. The companies, led by the Rockefeller-controlled Colorado Fuel and Iron Company, would not deal with the union. The companies suppressed attempts at organization, using blacklists, discharges, spies, armed guards, and the aid of venal state and local officials.

The miners wanted union recognition, a higher and firm wage, an eight-hour day, a union man as check weighman, the right *not* to buy at the company store, and the abolition of the "criminal" guard system. The operators refused.

In September nine thousand miners struck. They left the company hovels for tent camps set up nearby by the United Mine Workers. The company imported armed thugs who were deputized by the law enforcement officials. They dug rifle pits in the hills overlooking the tent sites and set up machine guns and searchlights. The company provided its guards with a specially built armored car, the "Death Special," which could be used to threaten and frighten the strikers.

The miners armed for protection. Some sporadic gunfire resulted in a few deaths on both sides. Yielding to company pressure, Governor Elias Ammons sent in the National Guard. At first the miners welcomed the protection. Then, when the militia sided with the company guards, the miners protested. The governor withdrew most of the National Guard, leaving one company commanded by Lieutenant Karl E. Linderfelt. Linderfelt's men poured machine-gun fire and rifle fire into the Ludlow tent colony. A boy and three men (one a militiaman) were killed. Next Linderfelt's troops poured oil on the tent colony and set it afire. Eleven children and two women were killed. Three strikers were murdered. The military fell back as the strikers advanced. In the ensuing ten-day battle forty-six people, most of them company guards, died.

President Wilson sent in federal troops. Later, court martials absolved the soldiers of any responsibility. Although Linderfelt was tried for murder, he got off with a light reprimand.

Rockefeller became the target of the outrage erupting across the country. He hired a public relations man from the Pennsylvania Railroad, Ivy L. Lee, to change his image. He also hired the former Canadian Minister of Labor, W. L. Mackenzie King, to figure out a way to improve relations with employees. Out of this came the Colorado Industrial Representation Plan, or the Rockefeller Plan, which called for a Joint Committee on Industrial Cooperation and Conciliation, and which gave the individual worker the right to appeal grievances from local officials.

The previous accounts of employer-union conflict point up some of the ways that were used to combat labor organizations. Counter-attacks by employers utilized a number of approaches and choices. One method the employers used was to propagandize in favor of the "open shop" and to say that this was the "American way" or the "American plan." In theory, the open shop is one that employs both union and non-union workers. In practice, the open shop really is one that is *closed* to union members. The cause of the open shop was taken up enthusiastically by employer groups and associations.

The National Association of Manufacturers, organized in 1895 to promote business, by 1903 was engaged chiefly in promoting the open shop. Other groups that joined the anti-union fight were the American Anti-Boycott Association, the National Metal Trades Association, the National Founders' Association, and the Citizens' Industrial Association.

Armed guards and hired thugs were used ruthlessly against union sympathizers; strike breakers were imported; labor spies infiltrated unions and plants; blacklists were used to bar unionists and union sympathizers from employment. Newspaper ads attacking unions were placed, lobbying activities in the nation's capital and in state capitals were carried on. The injunction and the yellow dog contract were widely resorted to.

Philip Taft sums up in the *American Worker*:

Unions were combated by a combination of blacklisting,

espionage, strikebreaking, and company unions. The National Metal Trades Association established labor bureaus in major cities for compiling records of employees in the industry so the blacklist could be more effective. To promote the open shop, the National Metal Trades Association conducted "the investigation and adjustment of questions arising between members and their employees." This kind of activity consisted of using industrial spies in plants to disrupt labor unions and cause the dismissal of union activists. If a strike in the plant nevertheless followed, "the association assumed complete control over the settlement of the dispute in exchange for the strikebreaking services which it made available to the member." The association paid the cost of recruiting strikebreakers and the bonus needed to attract them.

Large companies could successfully combat a union, and small companies joined associations. In 1903 local groups of employers, manufacturers' associations, industrial associations, employers' associations, and citizens' alliances joined together to resist the demands of organized labor. They formed the Citizens' Industrial Association, with David M. Parry of the National Association of Manufacturers as chairman of the executive committee. Under the leadership of C. W. Post, the dry cereal manufacturer, the Citizens propagandized to halt the spread of unionism.

The period from 1880 to about 1930 was a repressive one. The courts were generally hostile to unions, and labor law was judge-made. The widespread use of the injunction, which came into use in the 1880s, illustrates both the hostility and the way in which the judiciary established basic policy, a function supposed to be the province of the legislative branch of government. Since many courts were involved, overlapping jurisdictions resulted in varying decisions and attitudes. In the repressive era, however, the courts were on the side of property and property owners. The injunction protected property.

An injunction is a court order prohibiting a party from taking a specified course of action. Sanford Cohen (*American Labor*) explains that the court would issue an injunction to stop an action that might result in irrevocable damage to property in a situation where no other adequate remedy at law is available to protect the interests of the party seeking the injunction. Employers and judges quickly learned that the injunction was an ideal way to protect business interests in a labor dispute. Its impact was immediate and effective.

Injunctions were used to forbid picketing or other activities during a dispute. An injunction could prohibit the boycott of the goods or services of an employer whom the union considered unfair. It was an effective anti-union weapon; failure to comply with it could bring a fine or imprisonment for contempt of court, as occurred in the Pullman case where the injunction had a devastating effect on the American Railway Union.

The railroads had a stormy history of labor relations; the federal government made the first attempts at labor legislation in that industry. In 1898 Congress passed the Erdmann Act, providing for mediation and voluntary arbitration on the railroads (superseding an 1888 law). One section of the law dealt with the yellow dog contract. The yellow dog contract, which was widely used in the coal industry as well as in railroading, was an agreement, either oral or written, where as a condition of employment a worker agreed not to join a union or to leave the union if he was a member. It was a weapon against unionism, and the agreement was enforceable in the courts. The Erdman Act made it a criminal offense for railroads to discharge employees because of their union membership or activity. This section of the act, however, was held unconstitutional by the United States Supreme Court in 1908. A number of states also had laws forbidding discrimination for union membership; these laws also were declared unconstitutional, thus removing any legislative protection that union members had against discrimination.

The use of the yellow dog contract increased after World War I and adversely affected union organizing attempts. In the railroad industry the Railway Labor Act of 1926, which was held constitutional, did provide protection against discrimination for union membership. In private industry such protection—against yellow dog contracts and the easily obtained injunction—came with the Norris–LaGuardia Act of 1932.

Although many of the anti-union methods formerly used by hostile employers have been banned by law, some persist. Strikebreakers cannot be transported in interstate or foreign commerce (Byrnes Act of 1936), but they can be recruited locally. And in times of high unemployment, men and women desperately in need of a paycheck will risk the name-calling and the abuse and cross picket lines. Blacklists may not be maintained on computers, after all, discrimination for union activity is illegal, but nothing prevents personnel directors from telephoning or talking to each other and exchanging names of "trouble makers." Some employers and some unions use the services of armed thugs or have connections with various figures in crime and racketeering so as to enforce their control.

Other methods to combat unionization are to label all pro-union individuals as "radicals," "agitators," "foreigners," or "outsiders." Any concepts or activities that are disapproved need only to be called "un-American," "communist," or "radical" to be automatically negated. As we shall see in Chapter 12, racial, national and religious differences can be played upon to divide people and to set them against each other. These methods, used to particular advantage during World War I and the 1920s, and which are emotional rather than logical, are still used now.

The build-up of giant corporations in the last decades of the nineteenth century led to fears about trusts and monopolies dominating American industry. In 1890 the Sherman Anti trust Act was passed. It was directed against illegal trusts or conspiracies in restraint of trade and monopolies, and it gave the attorney general power to obtain injunctions or start criminal proceedings against violators. Injured parties could initiate civil suits for triple damages against violators of the act, and thereby hangs the case of the Danbury Hatters.

As a result of a dispute with D. E. Loewe and Co., a manufacturer of men's hats in Danbury, Connecticut, the United Hatters Union (AFL) called a strike and instituted a boycott, urging dealers not to handle the hats and customers not to buy them. The company estimated its losses at eighty-eight thousand dollars. Loewe, egged on by the American Anti-Boycott Association, sued under the Sherman Act and asked triple damages of two hundred and forty thousand dollars, a large sum for 1902. The case dragged through the federal courts, but in 1908 the Supreme Court held that the Sherman Act applied to unions. The case then went to trial; the union was found guilty, and a judgment of over two hundred fifty thousand dollars in damages was awarded the company.

The union could not pay. The homes and bank accounts of the hatters had been seized by court order since 1903. The American Federation of Labor appealed for funds and asked union members to donate one hour's pay. The judgment was paid and the homes of the hatters were saved. The union, however, was broken.

Fearing a flood of similar decisions applying to strikes as well as to boycotts, the unions turned to Congress for relief. During the Wilson administration, Congress passed the Clayton Act, two sections of which dealt with labor and seemed to promise a remedy against the application of the Sherman Act to unions. Rejoicing was premature; a 1921 decision of the Supreme Court said nothing in the Clayton Act protected unions against injunctions brought against them for restraint of trade. In one of the Coronado Coal cases involving the United Mine Workers, the court stated that unincorporated associations such as labor unions could be sued and held subject to triple damages. The question of the application of the Sherman Act to unions is still open. Supreme Court decisions in the 1940s virtually exempted labor unions, but in recent years the issue of application of the act has again arisen.

* * *

In the years just before World War I, the somewhat conservative AFL was strongest in the eastern part of the country. Gompers was intent upon showing that labor unions were responsible and respectable. In the West a more radical labor organization was developing.

The Western Federation of Miners had helped to establish the Western Labor Union and the American Labor Union. In the East the Socialist Trade and Labor Alliance was formed. In 1905 these groups united into the Industrial Workers of the World, one big union. The Wobblies, as they called themselves, advocated the abolition of capitalism and the formation of industrial unions.

By 1912 the Industrial Workers of the World had moved eastward, appealing to the foreign-born, the low wage workers, as it had previously appealed to the migratory workers in the western wheat fields and lumber camps of the northwest. By then, too, the followers of the Socialist Labor party had left or been driven out; the Wobblies became an association of migratory workers with a anarcho-syndicalist orientation. They won several strikes; one of the more dramatic was in Lawrence, Massachusetts, in 1912. There, the United Textile Workers, which represented a small number of skilled workers, would not help the mill hands protesting wage decreases. Most of the mill hands were immigrants.

The Wobblies responded and set up an efficient strike organization. Strike leaders were arrested; martial law was proclaimed, and the police reacted violently, clubbing women and children. Protests arose from across the country, and company officials agreed to meet with the union; the strike was settled. The Industrial Workers of the World, however, failed to follow up its initial victories with lasting organizations. They lacked the ability to build a permanent organization.

That inability, plus the Industrial Workers of the World opposition to World War I, resulted in the complete destruction of the Wobblies. They had always been anti-war; their men refused to register for the draft, were accused of hampering the war effort, and were the targets for vigilante groups who resented them. Their leaders were indicted in 1917 under wartime espionage laws and were imprisoned. Members were rounded up by the hundreds and imprisoned both during and after the war years. Their leader, Big Bill Hayward, jumped bail after he was convicted and fled to Soviet Russia where he died in 1928.

Had not World War I intervened, the Industrial Workers of the World might have become a powerful organization of the unskilled and the semi-skilled.

CHAPTER 4

Two World Wars

Before the United States entered World War I the American Federation of Labor numbered about two million members. When the war ended, the count had more than doubled. Economically, labor was in a favorable position. Immigration had slowed down to a trickle, so Americans did not face competition from new arrivals who would work for low wages. The demand for goods, particularly the materiel of war, kept plants and factories running at full speed. With the conscription of young men for military service, women took their places in the work force, an occurrence to be repeated during World War II, and a factor to have its influence on the women's movement.

From labor's point of view, some hopeful signs were apparent. Public attention had been focused on horrendous working conditions by the 1911 Triangle Shirtwaist Company fire in New York City in which about one hundred and fifty workers, mostly young women, were killed. The factory commission which sprang from the tragedy pressed the state legislature to pass the first serious safety laws for working people. Another tragedy, the Ludlow

Massacre, Ludlow, Colorado, 1914, called public attention to the plight of workers and resulted in a presidential commission of investigation and some improvements in conditions. In 1913 the Department of Labor was established, with William B. Wilson, a former secretary-treasurer of the United Mine Workers, as the first Secretary of Labor. Wilson, who had been a Congressman, established the Conciliation Service as a separate division of the department in 1918. In 1915 Congress passed the LaFollette Seamen's Act, which improved working conditions for sailors. A year later the Adamson Act, establishing the eight-hour day on railroads, became law.

The laws, however, not only did not encourage unionization but also made it extremely difficult. Employers could obtain injunctions, enforce yellow dog contracts through the courts, and spend enormous sums to combat unions through strikebreaking, labor espionage, and propagandizing. The Clayton Act, which had been hailed as barring application of the Anti-Trust Act to unions proved useless.

Once America entered World War I, the unions assured the government of their cooperation (with the exception of the Wobblies, who remained steadfastly anti-war). A month before the declaration of war, union representatives met in Washington to pledge their unqualified support and to draw up a statement of labor policy. They asked that organized labor be recognized by the government as the representative of all wage earners—organized or not—and that labor be represented in all agencies determining or administering defense policies. Thus the unions voiced a principle—which was accepted—that labor be represented on government committees, a principle that government was to honor later in similar situations.

The assurances of cooperation, however, did not eliminate labor disputes. Discontent rang high in 1917. Strikes called reached forty-five hundred in 1917. On the railroads struggles for the eight-hour day had been initiated by the four major craft unions.

Negotiations with the lines were unsuccessful; the brotherhoods called for a nationwide strike on September 4, 1916. President Wilson went to Congress on September 2 and asked for an eight-hour law to govern railroad operations. He got it. The Adamson Act was in his hands and signed on September 3. The brotherhoods knew the law would be challenged by the railroads and demanded it be put into effect on January 1, 1917. (With America's entry into World War I expected, the unions knew they could not strike.) Three members of the Council of National Defense, including Samuel Gompers, chairman of its labor committee, met with the rail union heads, who agreed to the eight-hour schedule just a day before the U.S. Supreme Court said it was constitutional. In December 1917 the federal government took over the railroads. Discrimination for union membership was not permitted; wages were set by a government board.

The general labor discontent, however, led to the establishment of the National War Labor Board, made up of management and labor representatives. No strikes and no lockouts were pledged for the duration of the war. The right of workers to organize and to bargain collectively was recognized. Workers were not to be discharged for belonging to a union or engaging in union activities. In return workers were not to coerce others to join unions or employers to bargain.

Another statement of policy said that employers were not required to deal with union representatives who were not employees unless this had been the previous practice: A provision like this paved the way for the growth of employees' work councils which were rivals of trade unions. These work councils (also called employee representation plans or company unions) multiplied rapidly. Some were established by employers to avoid dealing with trade unions; others were established by award of government boards as an expedient compromise.

During 1917 the Wobblies, who were still against the war, led a strike in the copper mines of Bisbee, Arizona. According to *The*

American Worker, the vigilantes rallied in Bisbee to combat the "foreign radicals" who were fomenting the strike. The sheriff deported twelve hundred strikers in freight cars to the desert without food or water. The mine owners eventually had to pay a million dollar settlement.

The great expectations for labor during the war were soon dispelled once the war as over. Even the limited protection of wartime policies ended. Strikes and lockouts grew; the postwar peak of over five million union workers declined rapidly in the aftermath of the wage cuts and anti-union drives of the twenties.

In Seattle, Washington, one of the first in a wave of postwar strikes involved the entire city. A general strike was called there in February 1919 in support of the striking metal trades workers in the shipyards. Food kitchens and milk stations were set up and people went about their business (the crime rate actually was lower than usual during the strike). The strike lasted less than a week, but was suppressed.

One of the first strikes by public employees occurred in Boston that same year. Calvin Coolidge emerged as the hero who smashed the strike. (In 1920 he was elected vice-president and became president upon the death of Warren G. Harding.) The Boston Police strike grew out of failure of a plan for adjusting working conditions and wages. The police struck on September 11, 1919. Twenty-four hours of looting, rioting, and violence ensued. Governor Calvin Coolidge sent in the National Guard, five thousand militiamen, to keep order. Eight civilians were killed in the clashes between roving mobs and soldiers. By September 14 the strike was over.

The major strike of 1919, however, was another defeat in the saga of the attempts to organize the steel industry. The AFL regarded the absence of a strong union in that industry as a symptom of a weak labor movement. In 1918 the AFL convention endorsed a plan by twenty-four unions with jurisdictions in the industry to campaign for unionization. The campaign was successful; thousands of steelworkers signed up. But obtaining industry recognition and collective bargaining rights was a different story. The chairman of the board of U.S. Steel, Elbert Gary, refused to meet with a union committee. The strike call for September 22, 1919, brought out three hundred sixty-seven thousand steelworkers.

Conditions in the mills were dismal. Wages were low for both the unskilled and the semi-skilled although the industry boasted about high wages and a welfare program. Most workers put in a twelve-hour day, six days a week, although in the nearby unionized mines the eight-hour day, forty-four hour week, was standard. The high wages were paid to a minority of highly skilled workers.

Taft reports that confrontations between strikers, private guards, and the local police began immediately. Local officials suppressed strike meetings. Gary remained adamant; U.S. Steel did not deal with unions. During the strike, one of the bloodiest of the time, twenty people, eighteen of them strikers, were killed. U.S. Steel would remain an open shop for another seventeen years.

Thomas R. Brooks' picture in *Toil and Trouble* is vivid:

> *The jails were jammed with strikers. Terror ruled the steel towns. . . . The deputy police at Braddock, Pennsylvania, attacked a funeral procession from ambush, clubbing the mourners into flight. . . . The parishioners of a Catholic priest sympathetic to the strike were mercilessly clubbed one Sunday after leaving services. Industrial spies whispered stories of Italian defections into Serbian ears and of Serbian back-to-work movements into Italian ears. In mid-October giant posters appeared on steel town streets proclaiming the failure of the strike and with a giant Uncle Sam, finger pointing at the looker from over the smoke of a steel mill, shouting, 'Go Back to Work,' . . . in seven different languages. Negro strikebreakers were imported to fan the flames of racism and break striker morale.*

The strike was broken. Perhaps expecting twenty-four unions to bury differences and rivalry was asking too much.

In the midst of the steel strike, President Wilson called a conference of labor, management, and public representatives to work out methods to promote industrial peace. The result was just the opposite. Gompers submitted an eleven-point resolution, one of which was the right of workers to organize and bargain through outside unions. The employer group countered by stating that employers had the right to deal or not deal with men or groups who were not their employees. In effect, employers would accept collective bargaining only through company-controlled organizations. (The public members straddled the fence.) As could be expected, the conference broke up.

Out of this conference came the strong movement of the 1920s to destroy unionism. In *American Labor Unions* Florence Peterson states: "Manufacturers' associations, boards of trade, chambers of commerce, builders' associations, bankers' associations, so-called 'citizens' associations', and even a farmers' association—the National Grange—united in a program, which they called the 'American Plan,' to save workers from 'the shackles of organization to their own detriment.' Open-shop organizations were established in practically every industrial center in the country. In addition to conducting 'patronize the open-shop' campaigns, these organizations extended direct aid to employers such as maintaining blacklists of union members and furnishing money, spies, and strikebreakers to employers involved in strikes."

Company unions, which employers did find acceptable, had developed earlier and multiplied. Large employers had paternalistic plans (corporate welfarism) under which they helped employees by supporting low mortgage rates, subsidized lunches and other meals, encouraged thrift or savings plans, established profit sharing and stock ownership plans. Some had grievance procedures under which an employee could present a complaint, but the final decision was the employer's.

How widespread were the uses of strikebreakers, spies and the utilization of anti-union propaganda? Brooks reports that it cost the Erie Railroad two million dollars for the services of Pearl Bergoff, the chief of a strikebreaking agency, to smash the 1920 strike of switchmen. The dues and the initiation fees of the National Metal Trades Association increased from $127,696 in 1918 to $541,236 in 1921 as employers sought the NMTA's blacklisting, spy and strikebreaking services. The membership of the International Association of Machinists, target of the NMTA, dropped from 330,800 in 1920 to 77,900 in 1924.

When the twenties began, unions had over five million members. By 1924 the membership had dropped to about three and a half million, and this decline continued until 1933. Only with the encouragement of the new administration and the new laws could organized labor prosper; despite the economic prosperity of the 1920s, labor grew poorer in members and influence.

A number of reasons contributed to this situation. One was the strong resistance of employers. Another was the wave of nationalism sweeping the country. Immigration was restricted; in 1921 the national origin quota system was approved. Attorney General A. Mitchell Palmer was diligently rounding up alleged "radicals"; the Ku Klux Klan was expanding. Unions were labeled "un-American."

Another significant reason was the unions' failure to make inroads in the new mass-production industries. The AFL clung to the idea of organization by crafts, not industries. Gompers was an aging union leader; his successor, William Green, was conservative. In fact, observers of the labor scene agree that he probably was elevated to presidency of the AFL because he was not a fighter, but would subordinate his own wishes to those of the heads of the powerful craft unions in the AFL.

The individual unions had their own troubles. Racketeers found it profitable not only to hire out to anti-union employers but to set up their own union locals and extort money from businessmen.

Gangsters were used by both employers and unions—in the New York clothing industry and in the building trades, for example. The taint of racketeering, corruption, and underworld influence was never to be eradicated, despite the laws that eventually were enacted. Unions simply are too lucrative and tempting an area to be overlooked.

The International Ladies' Garment Workers Union barely survived an internal struggle of another kind, an attempt by communists to take over the union. The attempt was defeated but at great cost to the union, not only in money but also in members. The communist influence would haunt and embarrass the union movement through the 1940s.

The 1920s were the last years in which the government had a *laissez-faire* attitude toward employers' conduct of labor relations. In the twenties most courts were still hostile and the state and federal governments were largely conservative, but some indications of change were apparent.

Some states had had laws on the books making it a criminal offense to discharge union members or to deny employment because of union membership. A similar provision had been incorporated in the Erdman Act of 1898, regulating railroads. But in 1908 the U.S. Supreme Court had declared that this section of the act was unconstitutional. Further support for the employers' use of the yellow dog contract came when the Supreme Court declared that the Kansas anti–yellow dog contract law was unconstitutional. In 1917 the Supreme Court upheld yellow dog contracts and ruled that union attempts to organize workers who were parties to such contracts were unlawful.

The ease with which employers could obtain injunctions was a major bar to union activities. The Clayton Act, which had elated labor, soon proved valueless in the case of *Duplex* v. *Deering*, which reached the U.S. Supreme Court in 1921. The court ruled that nothing in the Clayton Act legalized secondary boycotts or protected unions against injunctions brought against them for conspiracy in restraint of trade. So the situation regarding the use of the injunction in labor disputes remained the same—very discouraging for unions.

The procedure itself was damaging to the union involved. The complainant (usually the employer) could go to court and ask for relief in the face of a property threat. The court could then issue a temporary restraining order to halt threatened action until a hearing could be held. Then a preliminary hearing took place, after which the judge could issue a temporary injunction. After a trial a decision was made whether to issue a permanent injunction.

The problem was that a temporary restraining order could break a strike before it got under way, before a preliminary hearing was held at which the union could present its case. Even if, after a trial, the union won the case, by that time the union could be dead.

As to property rights, the injunction had long been a way to prevent damage in situations where money damages would be inadequate, for example where the evidence is strong that machinery or equipment would be destroyed. Most labor disputes were orderly and no evidence existed that the strike or picketing would damage either the premises or the equipment. But many judges ingeniously defined "property" as "the right to do business," thus giving companies a technique for suppressing strikes and other activities necessary for union success.

Another strong objection to injunctions was their scope, which would prevent not only actions that might damage property but also *all other actions* that accompany a strike. One of the most sweeping injunctions ever issued was in the railroad shopmen's strike of 1922. Judge James Wilkerson of the federal district court issued a restraining order banning picketing, strike meetings, communications, and being in the vicinity of the strike unnecessarily. Among the long list of other forbidden acts was the encouragement of the strike by letter, telegram, telephone, or word of mouth.

Until passage of the Norris–La Guardia Act in 1932, the permissable area of economic conflict between labor and management was not defined by law and only vaguely defined by the courts. Some courts were tolerant of union activities, others were conservative. Courts tended to be sympathetic toward the right of management to do business without interference from employees.

The importance of the railroads in the era before jet planes and automobiles became our chief modes of transportation cannot be overemphasized. The transcontinental railroads opened the West to greater expansion; they also made possible the industrialization of America. In time of war they were indispensable for movement of men and material.

And, they were a focal point for labor struggles and for labor strength. The railroad brotherhoods came out of World War I with a membership strong enough to resist anti-union efforts. Despite yellow dog contracts, the rail unions flourished.

From 1917 to 1920 the federal government operated the railroads, and the railroad companies themselves were subject to regulation by law. Under the federal government collective bargaining had been encouraged and a system for settling disputes had been established. Congress had set up a Railway Labor Board, but strikes in 1921 and 1922 disclosed weaknessess in the board. Both unions and management, however, realized that some system for settling their differences was necessary.

Out of this realization—and Congress—came the Railway Labor Act of 1926, which applies now to both railroads and airlines (but not to trucking). The act was significant, not only to the railroads, but to private industry as well, since it was the forerunner of later legislation.

The act sets up procedures for determining union recognition, outlaws company unions, and bans discrimination for union membership and activities. It allows each side to designate representatives for collective bargaining. The Railway Labor Act paves the way for legislation applying to the private sector of industry, the National Labor Relations Act of 1935.

For a time the Railway Labor Act was considered a model, with its grievance and arbitration procedures, but current observers find many flaws in it. For one a proliferation of grievances can clog the machinery, and speedy resolution of differences becomes virtually impossible. For another during World War II the rail unions were able to get presidential intervention in their disputes with the carriers and thus could obtain settlements more favorable to them than those obtained through the recommendations of emergency boards under the act. However, although critics agree that new legislation is needed, none has been forthcoming.

From the point of view of constitutionality, the act also is important. In 1930 the U.S. Supreme Court, in an opinion written by Chief Justice Charles Evans Hughes, unanimously upheld the power of Congress to outlaw discriminatory labor practices. A railroad company had interfered with the right of its employees to self-organization and the Brotherhood of Railway Clerks sued. The Court ordered the company to disestablish the company union, to reinstate the Brotherhood until a choice by secret ballot could be made, and to reinstate employees who had been discharged for union activity.

In the midst of the Great Depression Congress passed and President Herbert Hoover signed the Norris–La Guardia Act of 1932. The importance of the act is that it signals a major change in public policy from hostility and outright repression of unions to government recognition that workers have the right to negotiate the terms of their employment, to choose their own representatives for purposes of collective bargaining, and to be free of coercion or interference in their collective bargaining.

The statement of public policy contained in Section two of the act marks a completely new attitude towards unionism, one that was influenced by the severe depression as well as by a wish to remedy an imbalance of power between management and labor. The act:

1. Defines labor dispute as "any controversy concerning

terms or conditions of employment . . . whether or not the disputants stand in the proximate relation of employer or employee.'' The courts had previously interpreted a labor dispute as applying only to disputes between an employer and his employees, thus putting union leaders or organizers who were not employees completely out of bounds in their attempts to organize non-union companies. The new broad definition was upheld by the Supreme Court in several cases.

2. Makes yellow-dog contracts unenforceable in any court, thus virtually banning them.

3. Defines very precisely the conditions under which temporary restraining orders or injunctions can be issued. It prohibits, for instance, the issuance of injunctions against strikes; payment of strike benefits; peaceful assembly; picketing not involving fraud or violence; and advising, urging, or inducing without fraud or violence, the above activities.

Injunctions can be issued if:

a. Unlawful acts have been committed or will be committed and continued unless restrained.

b. Substantial and irreparable injury to the complainant's property will occur.

c. Greater injury will be inflicted upon the complainant by denying relief than upon the defendants by granting relief.

d. The complainant has no adequate remedy at law.

e. Public officers charged with protecting the claimant's property are unwilling or unable to furnish protection.

Although this act did little to minimize conflict or to encourage bargaining, it did wipe out the use of the injunction as an automatic bar to union organizing efforts. The bitter struggles in the coal fields, beginning with the massive strike of 1922 and the eviction from their homes of miners in Ohio and Pennsylvania who had struck in the summer of 1927, seems to have been a harbinger of the misery and deprivation that marked the early 1930s for millions of Americans.

Although a report from the AFL research department in February 1928 called attention to increasing unemployment among organized workers, neither the Labor Department nor the government saw any sign of the catastrophe ahead. At that time the government did not keep statistics on unemployment, but estimates were that heavy unemployment accompanied the prosperity of the 1920s. This persistence of unemployment during supposedly prosperous times should have sounded a warning bell; if it did, no one was listening. In May 1929 the executive council of the AFL recommended the establishment of a national employment service, a census to determine the number of the unemployed, and regularization of employment.

In 1928, Herbert Hoover was talking about poverty being banished from this nation; economists were telling people that prosperity was permanent. On October 24, 1929, the stock market crashed. The panic was incredible, but Hoover's response was to encourage business to be optimistic.

No systems of welfare or relief existed—no Social Security, no unemployment insurance, no Medicare, no food stamps, no Medicaid. Private agencies were supposed to assume the burden of providing food and shelter; hospital charity wards or clinics were supposed to provide minimum services. They strove to do so but were overwhelmed by the volume of demand.

Americans had always prided themselves on their industry and independence. Poverty was the fault of the poor. Anyone who really wanted to work could find a job. Thrift was a virtue. One was supposed to save for a rainy day or for old age. Children were supposed to care for their aged or infirm parents.

The Great Depression undermined these granite-hard principles. Unemployment and poverty were democratic. People who had saved diligently lost their savings as banks failed or used them up to pay for food and shelter as pay checks vanished. Prudent and industrious people lost houses and farms as mortgages were fore-closed. Unemployed professional and white collar workers joined day laborers as migrants on the road in search of any job. Shanty-towns or Hoovervilles sprang up as the homeless sought to eke out an existence. Over fifteen thousand men, most of them veterans of World War I, marched on Washington in the summer of 1932 to demand the payment of veterans' bonuses. Some of them set up a shantytown on the Anacostia Flats, near the Potomac. By order of President Hoover they were driven away by troops under the command of General Douglas MacArthur. Taft sums it up:

> *The absence of relief and welfare systems deprived millions of the bare necessities. Dire want forced them to seek assistance for themselves and their families, but none was available. State and local governments made some efforts to provide relief, until their budgets were exhausted. Pleas for federal aid were rejected by President Herbert Hoover, who insisted that the nation "had turned the corner." The attempts by Congress to provide aid were vetoed as a threat to the credit of the federal government.*

Sanford Cohen (*Labor in the United States*) reports that the new administration arrived on the scene and acted quickly, vigorously, and imaginatively. The new government in this time of severe hardship was guided more by the realities than by any economic philosophy. Attitudes had changed. Economic misfortune was a social failure calling for such efforts. In this new environment government had a positive attitude toward labor unions.

Of the numerous measures undertaken by the new administra-tion under President Franklin D. Roosevelt, one was a major law affecting labor organizations, the National Labor Relations Act (the Wagner Act).

The NLRA was a product of its time. If no Great Depression had occurred, if the faith in the wisdom of big business had not been shaken, if even the business community had not looked to the government for help, NLRA might not have been enacted in the form it then took. Labor itself was not strong at that time; union membership had declined sharply. But this new law, favorable to unions, grew out of the National Industrial Recovery Act of June 1933 an attempt to stabilize the economy and aid industrial recovery through the cooperation of labor and capital. Codes assuring fair wage and price levels were to be drawn up for each industry. Since the NLRA would encourage businessmen to join collectively in their own interest, the AFL and Senator Robert F. Wagner of New York, the key legislator, agreed that workers should have similar support from the government.

Section Seven (a) of the statute stipulated that every industry code contain the following conditions:

1. That employees shall have the right to organize and bargain collectively through representatives of their own choosing and shall be free from the interference, restraint, or coercion of employers of labor, or their agents, in the designation of such representatives or in self-organization or in any other concerted activities for the purpose of collective bargaining or other mutual aid or protection;

2. That no employee and no one seeking employment shall be required as a condition of employment to join any company union or to refrain from joining, organizing, or assisting a labor organization of his own choosing.

John L. Lewis of the United Mine Workers, which had been severely weakened in the twenties, saw his opportunity. Although he aimed at organizing the unorganized mass production industries, he first had to rebuild the United Mine Workers. He launched a tremendous drive, and the miners responded. An agreement signed in September 1933 with commercial mines, established the UMW as a power among American unions. But the "captive" mines, those owned by the steel corporations, refused to capitulate. The result was a strike, presidential intervention, and victory for the UMW. The significance was that the first wedge had been driven into the anti-union wall of the steel industry.

Although the law did not require workers to organize, unions were quick to seize the advantage. Sound trucks invaded the coal fields and the garment centers blaring forth the message that "the President wants you to unionize." Unions were formed in new areas, too, for example the American Newspaper Guild and the Screen Actors Guild.

Evidence is that the president was not as vigorous as was Senator Wagner in pushing for a permanent law. Wagner introduced such a bill into Congress in the spring of 1934. Industry was violently opposed to it. This opposition and the simmering conflicts over unionization in the steel industry led Roosevelt to defer action on the bill.

In 1934 the number of strikes and the violence accompanying them were enough to convince Wagner that the nation needed a new labor policy. The National Labor Relations Board, which had been created by Roosevelt's executive order, agreed. (The Board had been virtually powerless; employers opposed it and simply did not comply with its rulings.) Wagner's staff and the National Labor Relations Board worked out the bill that was introduced into Congress on February 21, 1935. Roosevelt did not support the bill strongly, but he did not intervene to delay it. Congress passed it with large majorities and the president signed the National Labor Relations Act into law on July 5, 1935.

In the meantime, between the introduction of the bill and its enactment into law, the National Industrial Recovery Act had been declared unconstitutional by the Supreme Court in May 1935. (The labor section of the NIRA, however, was not the basis for the finding of unconstitutionality.) Labor, by this time, was disenchanted with Section Seven (a) as it worked out in actual practice; the language of this section of the NIRA proved to be especially ambiguous regarding the status of company unions.

There was no doubt, however, that the National Labor Relations Act was favorable to labor and that its enactment was a victory for the cause. The statute states:

The inequality of bargaining power between employees who do not possess full freedom of association or actual liberty of contract, and employers who are organized in the corporate or other forms of ownership association substantially burdens and affects the flow of commerce, and tends to aggravate recurrent business depressions, by depressing wage rates and the purchasing power of wage earners in industry by preventing the stabilization of competitive wage rates and working conditions within and between industries.

The law seeks to redress this imbalance by protecting the right of workers to organize and by encouraging collective bargaining. The National Labor Relations Act has been amended by the Taft-Hartley Act of 1947 and the Landrum-Griffin Act of 1959, but it is the cornerstone of labor policy in the United States today.

The original law set up a three-man National Labor Relations Board with 1) the power to designate employee representatives for the purpose of collective bargaining and, 2) the power to prevent employers from engaging in unfair labor practices.

The board carried out its first function by determining the appropriate bargaining unit, that is, which jobs would be covered by a collective bargaining agreement and which employees were eligible to vote in a representation election. The elections were by secret ballot, and if the union won a majority of the votes, it was certified as the exclusive representative of employees in the unit.

The unfair labor practices by the employer, which the NLRB sought to prevent, were:

1. Interfering with, restraining, or coercing employees from self-organization and concerted activities in forming, joining, or assisting labor unions for the purpose of collective bargaining.

2. Dominating or interfering with a labor union (this bans the company union).

3. Discriminating among employees with regard to hiring or firing, wage rates and so forth so as to encourage or discourage membership in a labor organization.

4. Firing or discriminating against a worker who gives testimony or files charges with the NLRB

5. Refusing to bargain with the certified labor organization.

The three-member NLRB was appointed by the president and was given the power to make whatever rules and regulations it deemed necessary to carry out the act. It could hold hearings, issue cease and desist orders, or order action to be taken. Although it had no power to enforce its orders, it could petition U.S. Circuit Courts for enforcement of its orders.

The paragraphs above are simply a summary of the act, which left to the NLRB the enormous task of developing the procedures and the principles essential to its implementation. Over the years, through NLRB and court decisions, certain basic concepts have evolved. The later amendments to the NLRA and the decisions of the courts have resulted in substantial changes. It must be remembered that labor law in this country always is in a state of evolution, reflecting not only legislature changes, but changes in government administrations and in Board personnel, and changes in prevailing philosophies.

From its enactment the NLRA became a focal point for employer opposition. The anti-union walls of the corporations did not crumble at the blasts of union trumpets. Companies hostile to unions organized against enforcement of the law. They argued that the law was invalid and unconstitutional, and they tied up implementation of the Wagner Act for almost two years.

On April 12, 1937, in a five-to-four decision, the U.S. Supreme

Court upheld the constitutionality of the Wagner Act. (Five related cases had been reviewed by the Court, the most notable involving a steel company, Jones & Laughlin.) Justice Hughes wrote, in the majority opinion: "The fundamental principle is that the power [of Congress] to regulate commerce is the power to enact 'all appropriate legislation'. . . . That power is plenary and may be exerted to protect interstate commerce."

CHAPTER 5

Fireworks in the Labor Movement

More than one kind of explosion burst in the labor movement after passage of the National Labor Relations Act in 1935. Unionization expanded at a rate not experienced before, and the expansion often was accompanied by outbreaks of violence as the unions, encouraged by the new law, battered away at substantial anti-union resistance. Casualties accompanied victories. The movement itself was torn apart by the conflict within the American Federation of Labor and the emergence of the rival Congress of Industrial Organizations. Yet in the few years between 1935 and 1940 were what Neil W. Chamberlain in *Labor* calls "the golden age of American unionism."

> *It lasted for but a short spell, but in that brief time it developed a group of bold, imaginative, and able leaders who left their indelible imprint not only on the labor movement but on society. It turned American unionism from a narrowly centered craft-conscious nucleus into a broadly based movement. It demonstrated the importance of power in achieving social*

ends. It taught the labor movement that its interests were involved in virtually all social action and social legislation.
Within this brief period it racked up important successes. For the only time in its history it came close to seizing— perhaps even momentarily did seize—initiative and leadership in society from the business groups. But the pace could not be sustained. By 1940 internal dissension had divided Lewis [John L. Lewis] from his former lieutenants. The war years intervened to put a damper on labor activity.

The National Labor Relations Act gave labor an advantage it had never before had—the backing of the government. The federal law was followed by similar laws in many states, the ''little Wagner Acts.'' Yet the AFL did not appear to know what to do with the opportunity in its grasp. Gompers' successor, William Green, was by nature a compromiser given to placating the heads of many of the unions in the AFL, men who would not cede an ounce of power.

The opposition was led by John L. Lewis, the aggressive, ambitious head of the United Mine Workers, who held his union together through the twenties despite losses and setbacks. Physically, he was a cartoonist's dream; a big man, with a shock of black hair, bushy eyebrows, square jaw, cigar clenched in his teeth. He was well and widely read, an eloquent speaker who could quote Shakespeare or the Bible if it suited him. He also knew mines and miners.

The son of a miner, he went into the mines himself at the age of fifteen. His experiences, including carrying out the bodies of men killed in disasters, turned him into a fighter for mine safety. A union man, he rose from the ranks and was groomed by Gompers himself for a top spot in the AFL.

As early as 1933 Lewis was thinking about breaking away from the AFL. The question of craft versus industrial unionism came up at the 1934 AFL convention, where a meaningless compromise was agreed upon, but the issue really exploded on the convention floor in October 1935. Lewis then had the support of several other union leaders, including David Dubinsky of the International Ladies' Garment Workers Union, Sidney Hillman of the Amalgamated Clothing Workers, Max Zaritsky of the Hat, Cap, and Millinery Workers, Thomas MacMahon of the Textile Workers, Philip Murray, John Brophy, and Thomas Kennedy of the Miners, and the head of an old-line craft union, Charles P. Howard of the Typographical Workers. In November they were joined by Thomas Brown of the Mine, Mill, and Smelter Workers, and Harvey Fremming of the Oil Field, Gas Well, and Refinery Workers.

Lewis lost no time; on November 23 he wrote a note of resignation from his position as an AFL vice president.

The AFL Executive Council suspended the unions that composed the Committee for Industrial Organization in August 1936 and in November of that year the AFL convention expelled them. In 1938 the CIO declared itself a federation and changed its name to the Congress of Industrial Organizations. (Rivals for seventeen years, the AFL and CIO merged in 1955, bringing about eighty-five percent of organized labor into one federation.)

The rift grew out of a conflict of union philosophies and of personalities. The AFL unions, for the most part, were wedded to the idea that workers who wanted to organize would do so themselves; this was true of the skilled craft workers but not of the workers in the mass-production industries. The AFL leaders were old-line, aging leaders firmly set against industrial organization and all its implications. Green was a man who did not want to make waves. On the other side the leaders included many younger men like the Reuther brothers of the Auto Workers and Jim Carey of the Electrical Workers. Lewis bridged the generation gap; trained by Gompers, he remembered the old struggles but was energetic and astute enough to seize new opportunities.

The division in the ranks of labor actually rejuvenated the entire movement. The AFL was shaken out of its complacency and set about organizing aggressively. In 1937 the CIO had more members than the AFL; by 1940, the AFL had the edge.

When the CIO first came into existence as the Committee for Industrial Organization, most of the major American corporations were non-union. U.S. Steel, General Motors, Ford, and Goodyear Tire & Rubber were typical of the companies that were household words and in 1935 non-union. By the time the United States entered World War II, they had been organized. With their long history of opposition and hositility to labor organizations, their capitulation in just a few years was amazing.

The enthusiasm that propelled the CIO also evolved some new tactics, like the sit-down strike. The first major sit-down strike took place at the Goodyear Tire & Rubber Company in Akron, Ohio, early in 1936. The United Rubber Workers won recognition, and the victory was most encouraging to the CIO. The sit-down tactics would be used frequently in the next few years, notably in the drive to organize General Motors, a strike that some observers consider the greatest of the decade. (In 1939 the sit-down strike was ruled illegal by the U.S. Supreme Court.)

Lewis aimed at organizing the steel industry. He went after the old Amalgamated Association of Iron, Steel, and Tin Workers, which had been trounced time after time by the industry. Lewis wanted its industrial union charter, which had been granted many years before by the AFL, to lend legitimacy to the drive. On June 4, 1936, the Amalgamated joined the CIO and was merged into the newly established Steel Workers' Organizing Committee of which Philip Murray was chairman.

Irving Bernstein in *The American Worker* notes the threefold strategy of the Steel Workers' Organizing Committee: work with the ethnic groups that made up the labor force; exploit the work being done by the federal government, in particular the Senate's LaFollette Committee which was exposing anti-union practices; and capture the company unions from within. This last was extremely effective, especially with U.S. Steel. Lewis and Myron C. Taylor, chairman of the board of U.S. Steel, had secret talks that culminated in the signing of an agreement on March 2, 1937. U.S. Steel thus gave in without a shot being fired. Some believe that

Taylor was not as resolutely anti-New Deal as were other industrialists. Moreover, production in the steel industry was just picking up again; interruptions in production would not have made good business sense.

For a time it seemed that Steel Workers' Organizing Committee could move ahead without a hitch. Indeed, many smaller firms did sign up. By April it had a membership of two hundred and eighty thousand. Jones & Laughlin, however, balked and challenged the constitutionality of the Wagner Act. They lost; a National Labor Relations Board election followed; the union won and an agreement was signed. The company also had to reinstate the employees it had fired for union activity.

"Little Steel," however, was a different matter. These companies—Bethlehem, Republic, Inland, Youngstown and National —were bitterly opposed to unions. With the exception of Inland, their officers, led by Tom Girdler of Republic, were committed to the use of violence. When orders for steel fell off in the recession of May 1937 they welcomed a walkout as a test of strength they expected to win.

Girdler forced Murray into a strike for which SWOC was not prepared. By spring about seventy thousand men were out, and much violence occurred, with its climax in the Memorial Day Massacre of 1937. According to the LaFollette Committee, the police, without provocation, fired on the pickets. Ten were killed and over a hundred injured. Similar violence and deaths occurred at other locations.

The Steel Workers' Organizing Committee was defeated. Lewis looked to the president for help, but the president's refusal to support SWOC in the Little Steel Strike led to a break between the union leader and the president. In 1940 Lewis endorsed Wendell Wilkie for president.

SWOC then changed its methods and tried to get recognition through National Labor Relations Board proceedings and the courts. Before Pearl Harbor, the Steel Workers' Organizing Committee had won bargaining rights at Republic, Bethlehem, Youngs-town, and Inland, but they could not agree on wages. Eventually, with the outbreak of war, the dispute went to the War Labor Board, resulting in the "Little Steel Formula," which became the board's basic wage policy.

If the Steel Workers' Organizing Committee and John L. Lewis had a relatively smooth course to follow in organizing U.S. Steel, the opposite was true in the automobile industry. The United Auto Workers, committed to industrial unionization, joined the CIO. Under Homer Martin, a former Baptist minister who was its president, the United Auto Workers had as its target the big three: General Motors, Ford, and Chrysler. The UAW had made considerable headway among the General Motors workers, particularly in Flint, Michigan, where most of the working population worked for General Motors.

This was also the time of the sit-down strike; the United Auto Workers took the technique to its heart; it soon had the largest manufacturing company in the world at a complete standstill. The strike actually had started in Atlanta, Georgia, then spread to other locations, including Flint, Michigan, the core of General Motors operations. In Flint the sit-down lasted six weeks.

Governor Frank Murphy called out the National Guard not to evict the strikers but to keep the peace. The United Auto Workers employed clever diversionary tactics, putting on demonstrations and centering attention on one plant while strikers took over another. For instance, while strikers, police, and plant guards were clashing at Plant Nine, a union task force captured Plant Four.

Governor Murphy involved Lewis, General Motors' top officials, Secretary of Labor Frances Perkins, and President Roosevelt in the situation. On February 11, 1937, an agreement was reached. The United Auto Workers evacuated the plants; General Motors recognized the union.

Agreements with other auto manufacturers, including Chrysler, followed. But Ford held out. Henry Ford was adamant in his hostility to unions. Harry Bennett, his lieutenant, headed up a squad dedicated to violently combating organizing efforts. In 1937 when Walter Reuther and other United Auto Workers men tried to pass out leaflets at Ford's River Rouge Plant, in Michigan they were set upon and beaten unmercifully. This was the "Battle of the Overpass," and it was described by the union men in graphic terms at a National Labor Relations Board hearing. The union did not give up and the auto maker completely reversed his policy in 1941. He negotiated with Philip Murray and agreed to a union shop, checkoff, and grievance procedure—the primary aims of a collective bargaining contract.

World War II gave labor and management no time in which to adjust to a completely new relationship. Collective bargaining is not an exercise for novices; most of the participants on both sides of the bargaining table were inexperienced. The Wagner Act, passed in 1935 and declared consitutional in 1937, may have been joyfully accepted by the unions, but management hostility persisted. And the unions were not united; the CIO and the AFL were rivals. The CIO claimed the new National Labor Relations Board was pro-AFL in its rulings; the AFL charged the Board was pro-CIO. Management criticized the act as pro-labor and pressed for its appeal or amendment.

Time was running out. The United States was involved in the war as the major supplier for the Allied cause. In this country opinion was divided. On the one hand were the isolationists (including Lewis) and the America First proponents. On the other hand were the communists, committed to halting or hindering production that would aid the Allies. They did considerable harm, fomenting plant unrest and strikes. (When Hitler turned on Russia in June 1941 they became vociferously anti-Hitler.)

Lewis supported Wilkie against Roosevelt in 1940 and exhorted his followers to do the same. He said if Roosevelt won, he would consider the result "a vote of no-confidence and would resign the presidency of the CIO." Labor did what it always has done in America; it voted as it pleased and Franklin D. Roosevelt won. Lewis tried to renege on his promise, but Sidney Hillman maneuvered him out (Hillman had supported Roosevelt). Philip Murray became the CIO president.

During the year before Pearl Harbor labor unrest was endemic. Ford workers had struck that April; the United Auto Workers struck Allis-Chalmers in Milwaukee; communists called a work stoppage at North American Aviation in Inglewood, California. In 1941 over 4,000 strikes occurred, involving 2,360,000 workers.

The government had to take action. By executive order the president established the National Defense Mediation Board. A tripartite agency, it had four labor members (two from the AFL and two from the CIO), four industry members, and three public members. The board's methods for settling disputes in defense industries were mediation, voluntary arbitration, and if they failed, fact-finding with recommendations, which could be made public.

The board lasted less than a year. It received a total of one hundred eighteen disputes. In most cases strikes already were in progress. The National Defense Mediation Board was successful in most cases in persuading the unions to end stoppages, but it collapsed completely as a result of conflict with Lewis.

Lewis, though finished as the leader of the CIO could by no means be counted out as undisputed leader of the United Mine Workers. At stake were the captive mines, and through them the steel industry, essential to the war effort. The main issue was the union shop, which Lewis had won two years before in the commercial coal mines. The United Mine Workers called out over fifty thousand miners on September 15, 1941. Secretary of Labor Perkins agreed to certify the dispute to the National Defense Mediation Board, and Lewis agreed to send his men back to work for thirty days.

The president appealed to the miners on the grounds of patriotism not to strike again. Lewis, angered, called a second strike, then agreed to send his men back to work on November 3 for fifteen days. But on November 10, by a vote of nine to two, the board ruled against the union shop. Tom Kennedy and Philip Murray, the CIO members, cast the dissenting votes and resigned. It was the end of the National Defense Mediation Board. Roosevelt himself entered the negotiations, to no avail.

Lewis called a third strike on November 17, but Roosevelt succeeded in getting both sides to agree to arbitration. Lewis, sure of the outcome, ordered his men back to work. Lewis was right; the award was what he expected, but no one noticed. It was handed down on December 7, 1941, the day of the Japanese attack on Pearl Harbor.

At this critical time the president convened a labor-management meeting at the White House. Participants were twelve top labor leaders (six from the CIO, six from the AFL) and twelve industrialists. They agreed unanimously that for the duration of the war strikes and lockouts would be banned. Disputes would be submitted to a government board. But they divided over the issue of union security, with employers insisting the board should have no jurisdiction over the issue and with labor demanding that the board have this right. Roosevelt cleverly sidestepped the disagreement, announcing that he accepted the two principles on which all agreed and stating that the new agency would have jurisdiction over all disputes.

By executive order he created the National War Labor Board on January 12, 1942. A tripartite agency, it would have twelve members equally representing industry, labor, and the public. Although most of its procedures resembled those of the National Defense Mediation Board, it could also issue final decisions. Its power was derived from that of the president as commander-in-chief.

On a case-by-case basis the War Labor Board established policies. One of these, which influenced collective bargaining even after the war, stemmed from the old dispute over union security, the union shop. As a compromise between the union's demand for a union shop and the employer's resistance, the War Labor Board came up with maintenance of membership. An employee was free to join or not join a union, but once in he had to maintain his membership for the term of the contract.

The WLB also formulated wartime wage policies, as in the Little Steel case. Its authority, however, extended only to the dispute cases that came to it for resolution. To acquire and hold labor in a wartime economy, some employers, union and non-union, were offering substantial wage increases as inducements. With wartime cost-plus contracts the government eventually would have to foot the bill. The president, therefore, urged and Congress passed the Economic Stabilization Act to maintain prices, wages, and salaries at the level of September 15, 1942.

A hold-the-line order of April 1943 resulted. Workers could receive merit increases and be promoted to higher-paying jobs, but other pay raises were halted. As a result, the money that would have gone into inflationary and costly immediate pay increases was channeled, with WLB's approval, into the fringe benefits now taken for granted—paid holidays and vacations, health benefits, retirement plans. The very term "fringe benefit" is derived from the fact that these were "fringes," not essential components of salaries or wages.

With a few notable exceptions, unions soft-pedaled activities during the war years and cooperated in the war effort. One challenge to the War Labor Board came from the non-operating railroad unions in 1943. When the wage increase they demanded, twenty cents an hour, was cut to four cents under the Little Steel formula, they threatened a strike on December 30, 1943; the operating unions joined the strike call. President Roosevelt ordered the army to take over.

John. L. Lewis had provided another challenge to the authority of the WLB in the spring of 1943. Although the soft coal miners had exhausted their entitlement under the Little Steel formula,

Lewis demanded an increase of two dollars a day and portal-to-portal pay (pay for travel time from the entrance of the mine to the working site and return). Lewis refused to appear at the WLB hearing; the strike started. The president seized the mines, naming Interior Secretary Harold Ickes as administrator.

The WLB denied the increase and referred the portal-to-portal issue to the parties. The miners resumed the strike. In the meantime Congress passed the Smith-Connally War Labor Disputes Bill. This gave the president power to seize struck facilities if the war effort were interfered with. (The president vetoed the bill, but it was passed over his veto.) The WLB ordered Lewis to sign the contract with the mine owners, but he refused; an irate president said he would ask Congress for authorization to draft the striking miners into the army. Another walkout by the miners took place in October, and the president again seized the mines. Ickes, however, did work out a settlement with Lewis under which the miners got a dollar and a half a day more, taken mainly in the form of fringe benefits.

Another demonstration that contempt for the WLB would be taken seriously had its humorous aspect. Montgomery Ward, the mail order compnay, in 1944 refused to obey a WLB decision backing the right of the Retail Clerks to represent employees. The government seized Montgomery Ward. Its head, Sewell Avery, made an unforgetable picture as he was carried out of his office by four U.S. Army soldiers.

During the war years union membership grew at a tremendous rate. By 1945 over fourteen million Americans were labor union members; the union proportion of nonagricultural employment had reached a peak of 35.8 percent.

World War II undoubtedly speeded up the integration of unions into American industry and forced employers, who were otherwise inclined, to accommodate themselves to the realities of collective bargaining. All this occurred in only ten years.

However, this period of the consolidation of union power was followed by containment—the Taft-Hartley and Landrum-Griffin Acts—and renewal—the upsurge of public sector unionism in the 1960s.

The restrictive legislation resulted from a number of post-war events. During the war, controls built up tensions within the rank and file; after the war a wave of strikes in major industries battered the country: in the maritime trades, railroading, coal, oil, auto, electrical, steel and telephone industries. Four and a half million workers were on the picket lines during the 1946 strikes.

During the postwar strikes, President Harry Truman also seized the railroads and threatened the strikers with conscription; the unions called the strike off. In meatpacking, too, the struck plants were seized by the federal government, an act that the CIO Packinghouse Workers termed "strikebreaking." The National Federation of Telephone Workers, a reconverted company union, showed its freedom from the company by pulling a number of militant strikes.

And then came the Taft Hartley Act of 1947. The act reflected the ebbing union influence and the rising influence of business in the first Republican Congress since 1930. While wartime exigencies and a Democratic administration had forced business to conform to new federal policies and laws on collective bargaining; business did not like it. Business interests had not ceased efforts to combat the law and to stem union power.

Many observers friendly to the cause of labor disapproved of abuses in the unions, such as undemocratic procedures, discrimination, racketeering, corruption, and communist influence. The legislative history of the act indicates that its specific targets were John L. Lewis, James C. Petrillo (head of the Musicians), the building trades unions, communist unionism and large-scale strikes of the 1945-1946 variety.

The intent of the law was to balance the NLRA's restrictions on employers with similar restrictions on unions. Labor denounced it as a "slave-labor law." President Truman vetoed it, but Congress overrode the veto, reflecting more accurately than the labor movement the public attitude of the times toward "big unionism." The law was more punitive than what the moderate majority would have preferred. Senator Robert Taft, who sponsored the bill in the Senate, became the backer of amendments to ease its impact, but the amendments never passed. Later, the Landrum-Griffin Act would amend portions of Taft-Hartley.

The Taft-Hartley Act spells out unfair labor practices that unions are forbidden, including a refusal to bargain collectively. It outlaws the closed shop, jurisdictional strikes, and certain kinds of secondary boycotts. In Section Fourteen (b) the law does something unusual in federal legislation; it gives the states freedom to override the federal statue by enacting or maintaining right-to-work laws. (Right-to-work laws prohibit not only closed shops, but union shops and maintenance of membership. Less than half the states have such statutes, and these are mainly in the South or are largely agricultural. Texas, which has a right-to-work law, is the only one that has become heavily industrialized and will certainly be a target for organization.)

The original Taft-Hartley Act also contained a requirement that union officers sign a noncommunist affidavit. This requirement was later dropped.

The new law changed the National Labor Relations Board from a three-member body to a five-member one and created a new post, General Counsel, with final authority to investigate charges and issue complaints of unfair labor practices.

The Federal Mediation and Conciliation Service was set up as an independent agency; previously, the Department of Labor had a Conciliation Service. Another provision provides somewhat cumbersome procedures to be followed in national emergency disputes.

Although labor was bitter in its reaction to Taft-Hartley, the stronger unions did not seem to suffer from it. The weaker unions apparently were hurt more; the Textile Workers found the free speech provision an obstacle to organizing efforts in the South. The very unions against whom the law was aimed were not seriously hurt—the building trades, miners, musicians. But the enactment of Taft-Hartley brought unions into federal and state politics.

Government control over unions was one force impelling the AFL and the CIO to re-examine their division and to emerge in December 1955, as one labor federation. With the deaths in 1952 of William Green and Philip Murray within a few days of each other, George Meany became president of the AFL and Walter Reuther of the CIO. Meany had been head of the Plumbing and Pipefitters' Association, an old-line AFL craft union; Reuther had been the UAW organizer beaten up by Henry Ford's men in the "Battle of the Overpass." The passing from the scene of the two older men and the accession of the two younger ones made it possible for both federations to contemplate merger.

The older AFL union leaders had regarded the CIO as upstarts; the CIO saw the AFL as unduly preoccupied with protecting vested jurisidictional interests. But from December 1952 on, merger was the intent. For the first time the AFL was offering the CIO partnership, not absorption. Meany's personality and style of leadership were important to the merger.

The merger also came at a time when both the AFL and the CIO considered the Eisenhower administration as hostile to the interests of organized labor. Moreover, in the 1950s, expansion of one AFL union often was at the expense of another CIO union, and vice versa.

Also, as the dust settled in the forties, the various spheres of influence of the unions appeared to be more distinct; much of the earlier force of the conflict between craft and industrial union had evaporated. Internal affairs within both AFL and CIO had been straightened out; the CIO had purged itself of communists; the AFL had expelled the Longshoremen for racketeering and corruption.

In 1954 the AFL and CIO signed a no-raiding agreement. On February 9, 1955, the AFL and CIO met to approve an agreement for their merger. On December 5, 1955, the new federation, AFL–CIO was founded, bringing together about sixteen million workers. Meany was president and Reuther a vice-president and head of the newly created Industrial Union Department.

A few years after the AFL-CIO merger, Congress passed the Landrum-Griffin Act largely a response to disclosures of corrupt and undemocratic union action. It is a catch-all labor statute. The first five articles deal with union reform, providing for periodic secret elections of officers, a bill of rights for union members, detailed financial reports and disclosures by unions, and protection against improper trusteeships of unions. It bars communists from union office and also bars persons convicted of certain crimes until five years after termination of imprisonment for the specified crimes. (The bar on communists was held unconstitutional in 1965.) In addition it amends the Taft-Hartley Act.

Some excerpts from the act (Labor-Management Reporting and Disclosure Act of 1959) may indicate its objectives.

> . . . *to accomplish the objective of a free flow of commerce it is essential that labor organizations, employers, and their officials adhere to the highest standards of responsibility and ethical conduct in administering the affairs of their organizations. . . .*
>
> *The Congress further finds, from recent investigations in the labor and management fields, that there have been a number of instances of breach of trust, corruption, disregard of the rights of individual employees, and other failures to observe high standards of responsibility and ethical conduct which require . . . legislation that will afford necessary protection of the rights and interests of employees and the public generally as they relate to the activites of labor organizations, employers, labor relations consultants, and their officers and representatives.*

The new law, sometimes called the "anti–Jimmy Hoffa" Act, was aimed principally at the Teamsters and their president, James R. Hoffa. In 1957 Senator John McClellan of Arkansas headed a committee (to which Robert F. Kennedy was chief counsel) that conducted extensive investigation of union corruption and racketeering. Jack Barbash in *The American Worker* says:

The investigation established a pattern for several unions of personal aggrandizement and enrichment through racketeering, penetration of racket control, use of union funds for personal business, and conflict-of-interest transactions between employers and employer 'middlemen.' In union internal affairs the investigators found abuses in democratic processes including coercion and intimidation of dissenting members, election frauds and gross violation of members' civil rights.

Actually, labor had begun to sweep out its house before the Landrum-Griffin Act was passed. The Teamsters, for example, had been expelled from the AFL–CIO in 1956. The CIO had started to move against communists in 1949, expelling the United Electrical Workers and setting up the International Union of Electrical, Radio, and Machine Workers. The Farm Equipment Workers, the West Coast Longshoremen, and the Communications Workers were among the unions tossed out by the CIO. Some have since disappeared or their members have been absorbed by other unions.

How much effect the new law has had on elimination of racketeering is questionable. Its most constructive effect has been on union democracy, enabling members to challenge incumbent officers, and to register their discontent by turning them out.

The postwar years are associated with the laws asserting more control over labor unions and demonstrating management's hard line strategies. In doing so the significant progress made through collective bargaining during this period may be overlooked. Among the notable events were:

- 1950—UAW and General Motors negotiate a five-year contract with pension, escalator clauses, union shop, and annual improvement factor.
- 1954–1955—Four major unions, Auto, Steel, Rubber, and Electrical, propose the guaranteed annual wage. Later, this evolves into supplementary unemployment insurance plans.
- 1955—UAW and the Ford Motor Company sign a three-year agreement providing supplementary unemployment compensation.
- 1956—The Brotherhood of Locomotive Firemen and Enginemen, independent since its inception in 1863, affiliates with the AFL–CIO.
- 1956—UMW opens ten new hospitals in Appalachia, financed by UMWA Retirement and Welfare Fund.
- 1960—Pacific Maritime Association and the International Longshoremen's and Warehousemen's Union sign an agreement opening the way to relaxation of restrictive work rules and the increased use of labor saving equipment, in return for a fund guaranteeing job security.

Aside from the major legislation during this period affecting all workers, labor organizations started to accomodate to revolutionary technological changes.

Labor believes that employees have a stake in what happens to them as a result of changes in their working conditions, especially those resulting from technological progress, a situation which can deprive them of the means to earn a living. They believe that the employer has an obligation to ameliorate the adverse effects.

CHAPTER 6

The "New" Unionists

The "new" unionists are workers who have been around for some time, but for a variety of reasons they were not part of the main stream of organized labor until comparatively recently. These people are blacks, women, government employees, and professionals. In the last twenty years in particular they have become visible, vocal, and important members of organized labor.

Black and women workers suffered the consequences of a discriminatory society that excluded them from jobs and from the educational opportunities that would have prepared them for more demanding and higher paying positions. Government employees sometimes belonged to civil service associations, but these organizations were generally neither aggressive nor ambitious in the way a bona fide union can be. Professionals, white collar workers, and government workers had benefits not generally enjoyed by hourly wage workers.

Although the CIO in the 1930s organized workers, particularly in the automobile and steel industries, without reference to race, and although the United Mine Workers had had black members for some time, it was not until the civil rights legislation of the 1960s that black workers became part of the labor movement as a whole.

Yet the black worker in America has been on the labor scene much longer than many of the laborers who barred his way. The blacks came to the United States as slaves. The entire economy of the South was built on slave labor; many slaves were skilled workmen. Yet labor unions, which provided a means for many later immigrant groups to become Americanized, performed no such service for native blacks. A slave could not, as an immigrant could, save wages and buy a piece of land, or, when the West was opened, stake a claim on a piece of the new territory.

After Emancipation the freed blacks were left on their own. One-time field hands and domestic servants barely existed as share croppers and poor tenant-farmers, living a life of rural poverty until the 1940s. (With the 1940s and the shortage of manpower, many trekked north to work, exchanging rural poverty for urban deprivation.) Freed blacks who had some skills had to compete with whites for available jobs in the South; usually, the whites won.

The industrialized North ate up labor, but the labor that poured into mines, mills, and factories was immigrant labor, not black labor. For many immigrants joining a labor organization was a springboard not only into the industrial mainstream but also into the American way of life. Some already had union backgrounds or philosophies that embraced labor organization. From Scotland and Wales came miners who believed in unions. From Ireland came laboring men and women who knew what organization could do to the establishment. The European Jews from Russia and Poland often were skilled workers, imbued with the ideals of socialism, of bettering the condition of the working man. The needle trades unions actually were organized by immigrants; Samuel Gompers, the AFL's president until his death in 1924, was himself an immigrant.

Immigrants were shamefully exploited by employers and often used as strikebreakers to counter efforts at organization. National and religious differences were played upon to divide workers. Many unions were closed to all but native white Americans, but these bars were let down faster and sooner for immigrants than for blacks. Immigrants learned English; their children, born here, were eager to be American, fast to forget European connections. The ideal was the melting pot assimilation. But the immigrants were white—no skin tone immediately proclaimed their difference from others. Labor leaders were divided on immigration policy. Almost all favored exclusion of Orientals. Unchecked immigration, they thought, would depress wages. At the 1910 convention of the Socialist Party, restrictions on immigration were sought. The AFL for a time opposed limitations, but early in this century it favored an educational test. After World War I it endorsed the quota system. Then opposition was based on the adverse effect upon the labor market rather than upon race or religion.

In recent years, however, as the United States became a refuge for people who left oppressive regimes for freedom, many unions have played an important, positive role in helping these immigrants adjust to American work and American life. The International Ladies' Garment Workers Union, for one example, reflects many waves of immigration, from the Jewish and Italian workers of the early 1900s to the Hispanic, black, and Oriental workers of recent years. It conducts classes for learning English, for becoming citizens, for exercising their rights under our laws. Newspapers, bulletins, and educational aids are published in several languages.

It was not until World War I slowed immigration to a trickle that black workers were sought. Recruiting agents for northern companies traveled south in search of labor. Between 1916 and 1924 hundreds of thousands of black men and women moved north. Most of them were unskilled or semi-skilled; they filled jobs in meat packing, iron and steel, automobile and railroad industries. Rural people, they knew nothing about unions. Employers used them, too, as strikebreakers. During the steel strike of 1919, which led to defeat of the union, thirty thousand blacks were used as strikebreakers. Blacks were also recruited as strikebreakers in the 1920 strikes in meat packing.

The use of blacks and immigrants as strikebreakers reinforced existing antagonisms. Moreover, these groups (plus women workers), who were glad to work for any wage at all, threatened union efforts to maintain wage scales. These reasons, plus the irrationality of race hostility, excluded black workers from unions and prevented their playing significant roles in the American labor movement until recently.

Exceptions to the union policies of exclusion existed. The Knights of Labor did try to organize both black and white workers. So did the AFL carpenters and bricklayers in the South. The United Mine Workers took in both black and white miners, and black and white union members cooperated on the picket lines in mines and plants where both were employed. Another exception occurred in Alabama. When the unions of the state established the Alabama State Federation of Labor in 1901, they elected two blacks as vice-presidents.

Black workers were employed on the railroads in 1922. The six railway shop crafts agreed with the AFL Executive Council that black mechanics, helpers, and laborers would be allowed to become members of the International Brotherhood of Firemen and Oilers. The operating unions, however, excluded blacks. But it was on the railroads that the first significant association of blacks and unions began. In 1925 a group of black workers form the Pullman Company organized the Brotherhood of Sleeping Car Porters. Its first organizer, and then its president, was A. Philip Randolph, a remarkable man who devoted his life to eliminating discrimination by unions against black workers. The Sleeping Car Porters affiliated with the AFL. (Later Randolph and Willard Townsend became the first two blacks elected to the executive council of the AFL–CIO.)

During the New Deal era millions of blacks were unemployed and denied membership in many unions. It was during this same bleak era that millions of jobless blacks became the recipients of relief without discrimination, through the Federal Emergency Relief Act and later the Works Progress Administration.

With the wartime economy the prospect of employment in defense industries held out the prospects of jobs for blacks. A. Philip Randolph saw his opportunity. He developed the idea of a Negro march on Washington, which was scheduled for July 1, 1941. By May, Franklin D. Roosevelt was convinced that Randolph had strong backing and that the demonstration would be sizable. He tried to persuade Randolph to call it off (using Eleanor Roosevelt and Fiorello La Guardia, mayor of New York City as his intermediaries). Randolph refused. FDR invited him to the White House. Randolph informed the president that the march would be called off if FDR issued an executive order dealing with discrimination in defense plants. On June 25, 1941, President Roosevelt issued Executive Order No. 8802, which barred discrimination in defense plant employment and set up the Committee on Fair Employment Practices to hear complaints and adjust valid grievances.

Although blacks made progress, overcoming deeply rooted habits of wrongful discrimination was extremely difficult. The new CIO industrial unions accepted black and white workers on an equal basis, but this statement really is an oversimplification of what actually occurred within the unions.

The American Federation of Labor had from its inception the policy of admitting workers without regard to race or religion, but its affiliated national unions often had other ideas. For instance, the International Association of Machinists was founded in Atlanta, Georgia, in 1888. It offered membership to whites only. Samuel Gompers was eager to have the Machinists affiliate with the AFL, and he addressed the convention in 1893, telling them the "whites only" provision was wrong and had to be deleted. This union, founded in the South, refused. In the one year, 1895, that Gompers was out of office, the International Association of Machinists was admitted to the AFL.

The AFL dealt with the problem of organizing black workers,

especially in the South, by chartering separate local unions and separate central labor bodies composed of blacks. A number of national unions affiliated with the AFL followed the same policy. Gompers, opposed to segregated locals, nevertheless accepted them; otherwise, no unions could be established in the South. It must be remembered also that affiliated unions could practice discrimination because the AFL constitution permitted autonomy. The AFL feared that these unions would withdraw from the federation if subjected to pressure.

The AFL eventually discontinued chartering racially segregated central labor organizations. However, in the thirties, over twenty-five unions barred blacks from membership, the operating rail unions among them. The 1940s not only saw more jobs open to blacks but also a tremendous migration of blacks from the rural areas of the South to the urban areas of the North.

As the black workers moved north and into jobs in major industries such as steel, automobile, and meat packing, they also moved into the areas which the new CIO was organizing. They were taken into these unions, which had no color bars. The successful organization of industrial unions by the CIO jogged the AFL into action. Many AFL unions started to take in unskilled and semi-skilled workers whom they previously had scorned.

The wartime ban on discrimination in defense industries, the abolition of segregation in the armed forces (by President Harry Truman), the passage of anti-discrimination statutes by some states and the rising tide of enlightened public opinion, plus unremitting pressure from civil rights organizations and activists, led in 1964 to the passage of the Civil Rights Act.

By now the AFL and CIO had merged. To the credit of the federation was its active support of civil rights legislation. George Meany, head of the AFL–CIO, was among those who were adamant that the act contain a job rights provision. President John F. Kennedy, in whose administration the legislation was first formulated, had feared that a job rights section would jeopardize the passage of the legislation. The original act sent to Congress by the Kennedy administration did not prohibit discrimination in employment. Kennedy's tragic death brought Lyndon Johnson to the presidency. One of his objectives was to move the civil rights bill that was tied up in Congress.

The legislation was passed, and it included Title VII banning discrimination by both employers and unions. The AFL–CIO mobilized its facilities to bring its affiliates into conformity with the letter and spirit of the law. It would be satisfying to report that with the support of the law and the federation that discrimination has been eliminated from the labor movement.

Not so. Today, almost twenty years after Title VII, the discriminatory practices persist. In August 1982, for example, a Federal District Court held a sheet-metal local and a group of 121 companies in contempt of court for willful disobedience of an affirmative-action order to increase the number of nonwhites. A fine was imposed. Among the actions by unions and employers that had violated the affirmative-action order was an apprenticeship program retarding the entry of nonwhites, authorizing white members of out-of-town locals to work in New York instead of expanding membership, and an agreement between union and employers that one of every four journeymen on a job be fifty-two years of age or older. Since these older workers were all white, the effect of this agreement would be to discriminate against nonwhites.

As blacks and other minorities (Hispanic, for example) have sought to get into the building crafts, they have resorted to demonstrations, frequently violent. Positive outreach programs, which actively recruit, train, and place minority workers, have been developed. Programs have been developed in Chicago, Philadelphia, Boston, and New York. However, jobs must also be available, and unless the construction industry is healthy, these efforts cannot be entirely successful.

Another area of concern to blacks and other nonwhite union members is representation in union leadership. The representation of racial or other minorities in union hierarchies has trailed behind their numerical strength. This was a source of difficulty for the UAW in Detroit and in other unions such as those in steel and transportation. One of the reactions to the situation has been the development of black caucuses within the auto, steel, and teachers, unions. And as a result of black activism as well as a recognition of realities, unions have elected and appointed more blacks to positions of union leadership.

The attitude of labor unions and employers toward women reflected accepted views of society. Although the Knights of Labor opened its doors to women workers late in the nineteenth century, women generally were not in the forefront of the labor movement until later. They were not employed in the skilled crafts that constituted the core of the early unions nor were they employed in industries such as railroading, coal mining, or printing.

With the industrialization of the United States, women and girls worked in factories and mills. While they were concerned with the strike in Lawrence, Massachusetts, in 1912, they were generally ignored by the labor movement. The view was that they were in the labor market only temporarily; that, after working a short time they would marry, raise a family, and depart from the world of paid labor. Women themselves generally held this point of view. The woman with visions of a skilled job or a profession was the exception. Indeed, unions would have found it very difficult to convince women workers that organized labor had any advantages to offer them.

Some careers were open to women, mainly in nursing and teaching. But women in these professions viewed themselves as professionals, not as part of the laboring rank and file. If their pay or working conditions were less than satisfactory (often they were deplorable), they usually enjoyed community respect and until the 1960s preferred prestige to pay.

In wartime women were called upon to replace the men who had left industry for the armed services. They did a "man's" job and were lauded for their patriotic efforts. With the end of hostilities they were expected to vacate their jobs and return to hearth and home. After World War II, however, many were loath to do so.

One major exception to the relationship of unions and women occurred in the garment trades. Women in the needle trades joined the International Ladies' Garment Workers Union and struck occasionally. As grievances were eliminated they tended to leave the union. In 1909, however, thirty thousand waistmakers, seventy percent of them women, struck. The strike lasted fourteen weeks and ended with the strikers gaining contracts in over three hundred shops. The ILGWU, composed of both men and women in the garment trades, is one of the few international unions that always had substantial membership among women.

World War II gave blacks and women a chance at jobs that had not before been available to them. And this time neither group would go quietly into limbo once the emergency was over. Pressure for legislation banning discrimination began to build and rights organizations formed and fought for their cause. The women's movement also started to coalesce. The 1950s seemed quiet, even apathetic; but in the 1960s the accumulated pressures exploded into the full-scale civil rights movement and culminated in the Civil Rights Act of 1964.

The Civil Rights Act provided the statutory basis for combating discrimination not only for race, color, religion, and national origin but also for sex, thus opening a path for women as well as for black, Hispanic, Oriental, and other nonwhite workers, as well as for Jews, Roman Catholics, and members of other religious faiths differing from the Protestant majority.

For women the change was dramatic. In the generation after World War II, women's share of jobs rose from one quarter to nearly half. Married women with children accounted for more than a third of jobs, an increase from eleven percent in 1948.

In labor unions some of which never had a woman member,

women are still not represented to any extent at the highest levels, but the formation of women's trade union coalitions and caucuses will undoubtedly have an impact on the labor movement. For unions the increasing number of women in the work force presents a new opportunity for organization.

The juxtaposition in this chapter of black and minority workers, women, government employees, and professional employees in relation to labor unions is intentional, not simply a device for disposing of groups that did not fit neatly into two hundred years of labor history. It was in the decade after the last major federal labor legislation, the Landrum-Griffin Act, that as a result of social upheaval and legislative change these groups burst upon the national attention. They had been there all the time, of course, but the peculiar circumstances of the 1960s thrust them into immediate prominence. In a way the assassination of Dr. Martin Luther King united most of these diverse elements: civil rights, black workers, government unions. Dr. King was in Memphis, Tennessee, to show his support of a strike by public sanitation workers.

In Memphis most of the sanitation workers were black. The sixty-five-day strike arose out of a grievance and a race issue. One January day, when it began to rain, twenty-two black employees were sent home. White employees were not; when the brief downpour ended, they were put back to work and received a full day's pay. When the black workers complained, they got two hours' call-up pay. They called a meeting of their union, a local of the American Federation of State, County, and Municipal Employees. Then they struck on Lincoln's Birthday, which happened to be the next Monday.

The mayor said the strike was illegal. Eventually, what had begun as a walkout over a grievance became a strike for union recognition and a contract.

A rally was broken up by police with their clubs and Mace; the entire black community backed the union. The struggle drew nation-wide attention, and King went down to underscore its urgency. He was murdered, and the tragedy precipitated a settlement.

This incident is cited here because public employee unions have become increasingly involved with minorities: especially blacks and women. Particularly at state and local levels the low-wage workers—blacks, Puerto Ricans, Mexican-Americans—are being enrolled as union members. Many of the newly organized were once considered "unorganizable." Although the government unions have had significant success with professional and white collar employees, their major increases in membership have been with the blue collar groups in government.

In the years after Taft-Hartley and Landrum-Griffin union membership did not keep pace with the growth of the labor force in nonagricultural employment. The entire white collar field seemed unresponsive. However, there was an upsurge in the government sector reflected in the enormous expansion of employment at the state and local levels as well as in the federal government. Also, laws and executive orders encouraged collective bargaining. In New York City Mayor Robert Wagner recognized public employee bargaining in 1959; President John Kennedy issued Executive Order No. 10988 in 1962. Some states enacted their own collective bargaining laws for public employees.

Why the emergence of government unions in the sixties? Among the reasons that have been proposed are that the unprecedented expansion of government employment brought in many young people; not only did they have a more questioning attitude, but also they were more receptive to unionism than the older, more conservative civil service types. Questioning the establishment came naturally to those who came of age in the sixties.

Private industry also had made more progress in bringing personnel practices up to date; many government jurisdictions fell short of the mark. The advantages of benefits such as retirement plans, which the civil service employees once had and private sector employees did not, had evaporated. Salaries in government service were not comparable with wages in industry. The restlessness and dissatisfaction of the era of insecurity also contributed to the upsurge in government unions: the civil rights movement, the opposition to the Vietnam war, and student activism. What is amazing about government unions is their militancy or what is known as their brinkmanship. Their leaders have matched this spirit of militancy; they may not be lovable, but they are effective. The public may have been surprised to see nurses and teachers marching with picket signs or to see police officers and fire fighters engaged in job actions, but where politeness and patience once failed, the newer militancy has been successful.

Although strikes against the government have long been considered illegal, public employees have struck, often bitterly and for prolonged periods of time, for instance: the New York City transit strikes of 1966 and 1980, the strike by four Pennsylvania public unions in 1975 (the first statewide strike of public employees), teacher strikes which occur across the country just about every school year, the postal strike of 1970, and the air controllers strike of 1981. Despite anti-strike laws, fines, and other penalties the pace of public employee strikes has continued. (In New York where the 1966 strike of the transit workers violated state law, the legislature passed a law exempting the union members from penalties. The law was replaced with a new one, the Taylor Act, detailing collective bargaining and representation rights and procedures and providing impasse settlement machinery.)

In the federal sector two strikes can be mentioned as showing distinct approaches by different presidents to dispute settlement in the government. The postal workers who struck in 1970 (when Richard Nixon was in office) were in clear violation of the law forbidding strikes. According to the law, any postal worker who struck could be fired. The postmaster general was forbidden to bargain with strikers, and troops were called in to keep the mail moving.Eventually, the strikers were reinstated, with a pay increase, and got bargaining rights similar to those under Taft–

Hartley for the private sector. In return for denial of the right to strike, they got binding arbitration.

The air controllers strike of 1981 (Ronald Reagan's administration), ended with the union broken and its members fired from government service. The relative strength of the unions may have played some part in the disparate treatments. About half a million belong to the postal unions; under twelve thousand were with the air traffic controllers, and the supervisory staff could handle the workload.

These two instances stress one of the most important problems faced by unions in the public sector: the right to strike. In almost all government jurisdictions employees do not have the legal right to strike (Hawaii is one exception) but they do have the power to withhold their labor.

Many felt that without the right to strike, no true collective bargaining exists. Arbitrator Philip A. Carey, S.J., wrote in a letter published in *The New York Times*, July 26, 1966:

In days past, pay and working conditions for men and women in civil service were determined by legislative and administrative fiat. We have evolved from this stage of political serfdom, and we now plume ourselves that we share this decision-making with the working people themselves, through the process of collective bargaining.

If this is so, we have to go the whole way and assume all the consequences and dangers such a grant of power implies. If we assert that collective bargaining should be the policy of the state and municipality in their relations with the persons who work for them, we must agree to grant the right to strike.

For without the right to strike weapon (and, mind you, I hope that it will be used rarely and responsibly) you just do not have collective bargaining. You may have a close imitation. You do not have the reality.

The withholding of labor is not merely the ultimate force at

the bargaining table,where negotiations for a real and fair
agreement are threshed out. It is much more basic. The very
acceptance and existence of a labor agreement depend upon
the giving or the withholding of labor.

At this time, almost three fourths of the states (and several municipalities) have some statutes relating to bargaining by public employees (the others, where no such laws exist, manage by common law or ad hoc acts of the legislature). The laws are not uniform, so generalizations about them would be inaccurate. Comprehensive statutes, such as the Taylor Act in New York, usually state the right of employees to join labor organizations, tell how bargaining units will be established and the union representative chosen, specify the issues subject to collective bargaining, and provide procedures for settling disputes. Most prohibit strikes altogether; others spell out the limited circumstances under which a strike is permissible.

If the statutes of the states on collective bargaining by public employees are a patchwork, the federal government does have orderly procedures. Although unions in the federal service go back at least to the middle of the nineteenth century, they were effective more through lobbying than through bargaining. Presidents were generally firmly set against transferring collective bargaining from the private sector to the public; President Franklin Roosevelt, by the way, did not favor collective bargaining by public employees.

It was not until the administration of John F. Kennedy, who had labor backing, that any action favoring collective bargaining was taken. Executive Order No. 10988 issued in 1962, which provided for a limited collective bargaining, was the first recognition by the federal government that public employees had any right to join a union and bargain with their agencies. It had its deficiencies but was a start. Labor hailed it, and it stimulated unionization in the federal sector.

During the subsequent administration President Lyndon Johnson appointed a panel to review experience under the executive order and to recommend changes. Under President Nixon Executive Order No. 11491 was issued.

It set up a Federal Labor Relations Council, provided for a Federal Service Impasse Council, specified how a union could get exclusive bargaining rights. It also excluded units of supervisors from exclusive recognition except where historical precedence had been established. Later amendments to the Executive Order broadened the scope of negotiations. The amended Executive Order bears some resemblance to the National Labor Relations Act, but important differences distinguish bargaining in the federal government. The agency shop and the union shop are banned; government strikes are prohibited; wage issues are not negotiable; and other issues, such as promotions, discipline, and transfers are not negotiable. The reason is that the economic issues such as wages are determined by law, while issues such as promotion are subject to a combination of laws and civil service regulations. Grievance procedures and arbitration are permissible: The order says agreements between agency and a labor organization "shall provide a procedure, applicable only to the unit, for the consideration of grievances; and that arbitration may be invoked." However either party to an award may file an exception to it with the FLRC. No provision is made for final and binding arbitration, as in the private sector.

The great expansion of unionization in the public sector also included many professional men and women, especially teachers. But both inside and outside the public sector, professional people have been engaging in union activity. Many professionals belong to associations, such as the National Education Association or the American Nurses' Association, rather than labor unions. But in recent years these associations have had to become collective bargaining organizations and to behave like labor unions or lose their members to the unions. Not that professionals ever have been strangers to labor organizations: Actors' Equity, which struck the

New York theaters over fifty years ago and is part of the Associated Actors and Artistes of America; AFL–CIO, a union that also embraces the newer arts such as television; the Newspaper Guild is a union as are the Major League Baseball Players' Association, the Football League Players' Association, and the Hockey League Players' Association. Unions keep up with the times or perish, and the professional and white collar field is, along with the service trades, a source of new members.

Finally, the old age of the crafts and the new age of the professional seem to have linked up when the first union man set foot on the moon. He was Edwin Aldrin, a member of the International Association of Machinists.

CHAPTER 7

Union Structure and Operations

The heart of the labor movement in this country is the local union. Their numbers alone are an indication of their significance: over sixty-three thousand locals, according to the United States Department of Labor. Most locals are affiliated with national or international unions ("international" designates both nationals and internationals). In turn most internationals are affiliated with the federation, the AFL–CIO. Some locals are independent, unaffiliated. Some internationals do not belong to the federation. At present the two major internationals that are outside the federation are the International Brotherhood of Teamsters and the United Mine Workers.

In the United States the first unions were associations of craftsmen, and the term "craft union" still is used. Since the original distinction between craft and industrial union is important to understanding the background of the labor movement, definitions are in order. According to the *Dictionary of Industrial Relations* (by Howard S. Roberts) a *craft union* is an organization of workers bound by a common occupation, skill, or trade, or a group of closely related skilled tasks. An *industrial union* is a term used to describe the structure of a particular union in relation to company operation. Workers in an industrial union are organized essentially on the basis of the product.

Craft unions also are called horizontal unions and industrial unions are called vertical unions. For instance carpentry is a skill or craft. The union is the United Brotherhood of Carpenters and Joiners. Its locals are comprised of all the carpenters in a geographical area, although they are employed by different contractors. A union organized on the basis of a product or industry is the United Steelworkers of America. Its locals are organized on the basis of a company or a plant, and include unskilled, semiskilled, and skilled workers at that location.

The differences between the proponents of craft unionism and the proponents of industrial unionism led to conflicts and splits within the labor movement, including bitter jurisdictional disputes. Much of the antagonism between the AFL and the CIO flowed from their irreconcilable views over craft versus industrial unionism. The AFL bias toward the crafts was a major factor in the establishment of the CIO. (The influential personalities of William Green, AFL President, and John L. Lewis, United Mine Workers President, were other formidable factors.)

Rapid changes in industrial technology as well as the need for survival have blurred distinctions between craft and industrial unions. Most unions now are neither purely craft nor purely industrial. For example the electricians, as a craft union, cover electricians working in the building construction industry. They also have locals taking in various production workers in factories and plants.

The average union member is more concerned with his local than with the international union. It is the local that handles his grievances; it is at the local level that labor agreements usually are negotiated, and it is the provisions of the local agreement that determine his pay, his benefits, and other working conditions. Most locals are affiliated with an international union. Some are not; they may be chartered directly by the AFL–CIO; or they may be completely independent of any affiliation whatsoever. A new local union may start in a completely new industry or occupation. As soon as a few such locals get under way, they may combine into a new international union. The new international may become an AFL–CIO affiliate, or it may remain independent.

When a local is a subordinate of an international, its authority and its responsibilities are prescribed by the international. Through the local the international exercises its control over members. The international's constitution defines the role of its locals, although each local has its own bylaws. Usually, when a new local is to be chartered, its bylaws must be approved by the international before the charter is issued. Amendments to a local's bylaws also require approval. If a local violates any established rule of the international, it may be suspended or even expelled.

The local union's main duties are contract negotiation, policing the labor agreement to see that it is carried out properly, grievance processing, and where necessary, organizing and running a strike. Locals also may carry on educational and social activities.

A local is run by its officers and elected by the members. The election procedure, the pay—if any—of the officers, and the qualifications of candidates usually are spelled out in the constitution of the international. It is common practice to require candidates for office to be in good standing and to have been members for a specified period of time. Under the Landrum-Griffin Act locals must hold elections at least every three years by secret ballot.

The procedure for removal of an officer also may be detailed. (If adequate procedure is not provided, the Landrum-Griffin Act permits removal under specified conditions of any officer guilty of serious misconduct.) A grave violation of the international's rules may provide grounds for expulsion or removal from office. In some unions members can file charges against an official and demand investigation of the charges and trial of the accused. Further appeals may be made to the international union and, finally, the union convention.

Most local unions have a president, vice-president, and a secretary-treasurer. The size of the local, like the size of a company, determines its structure. In a small union the officers generally continue to work at their jobs. A larger and more complex union local may require full-time paid officers, even some paid staff members. In these cases a union office, especially that of president, carries a considerable amount of prestige and power. The incumbents are likely to make every effort to hold their positions—an effort often made more difficult now because unions now tend to be made up of many dissimilar groups, each of which has its own interests.

One of the differences between craft unions and industrial unions is that craft union locals, in addition to their officers, have a business agent, who is a full-time, paid employee with a great deal of responsibility for the daily operation of the local. Unlike an officer, his term is indefinite. Often, he was an officer at some time and has depth of experience in the trade or the industry. He provides continuity, gives advice, participates actively in negotiations, yet has no vote.

In the building construction trades the importance of the business agent is evident. Typically, one local represents all the members of a craft, who may be unemployed at a given time or working for many different contractors. The one unchanging point of contact with the local is the business agent. Should workers be needed on a job, the contractor lets the business agent know, and the latter supplies them. The business agent goes from location to location, sees that the contract is observed, and may even settle grievances on the spot. Some business agents collect dues, run the union office, get out a newsletter, and do the administrative chores. They may supervise a staff. The position can be a powerful one.

There are stewards in the craft unions too. The steward may be the first man on the job or the worker with the most seniority. He is chosen not elected. Stewards provide the day-to-day union representation; they communicate with the business agent, not with their counterparts on other jobs under the same labor agreement.

The stewards in an industrial union are elected by the workers in a department or in the company, if it is a small one. Usually, the stewards comprise a council, and all the stewards or all the employees may elect a chief steward. Each union steward sees to it that the contract conditions are enforced in his department. If no checkoff arrangement exists, the steward may collect dues. The main function of the union steward is to handle grievances at the first step or steps of the procedure. A secondary function, of course, is to provide a communication link between the union officers and the workers and, of course, with each other.

The council meets from time to time to discuss problems, exchange news, and perhaps offer advice to each other as needed. When new contract talks are in the offing, the stewards provide information about what contract changes may be desired by members or what contract changes they believe are required. When a new labor agreement is reached, the union officers usually describe it to the stewards first, depending on them to win over the members and so get the agreement ratified.

If a strike should be called, the stewards are expected to whip up worker enthusiasm and keep morale high. They serve as picket captains during a strike, seeing that their people do their stints of picketing at the right time and place.

Because an on-the-job presence of a union representative is desired both by the union and the employer, stewards generally are given superseniority; this means that if a layoff occurs in a department, the steward is the last person to be laid off. The steward's role may be further defined in the contract itself. Besides specifying his role in the grievance procedure, the time required for him to investigate and handle a grievance may be set forth. This time, which is paid for, may be limited to so many hours per week or per month or may be virtually unrestricted.

The requirement for regular meeting of a local ordinarily is given in the constitution of the international. One or two meetings a month is the common practice, although special meetings may be called if necessary, for instance, if a strike vote must be taken. The usual order of a meeting would be a reading of minutes of the last meeting, reports on finances and on activities, past and prospective.

Unions share with other kinds of organizations the problem of getting people to attend routine meetings. Members stay away and then complain that some measure to which they object was railroaded through. To avoid these complaints and to insure attendance some unions fine members who are absent from a specified number of meetings.

Other variations of locals deserve a brief mention. One is the amalgamated local, which is a large local covering all or most workers in a number of establishments in the same city or industry. These amalgamated locals may have several branches consisting of the workers in each industry. Each branch elects its own stewards or bargaining officials and may hold its own meetings.

Other local forms of organization are joint boards or district trade councils. These consist of locals that have jurisdiction within related trades or industries. Their aim is to provide a united front in bargaining and uniformity in working conditions among companies in the same industry within a city or geographical area.

Some internationals require their locals to set up a joint board or council when more than a given number of locals exist in an area, and then require all the locals to join. Their powers and functions differ; some are governing bodies; some are advisory. Some can negotiate a citywide agreement and some can call citywide strikes. Delegate groups composed of locals from the same international are called joint boards most of the time; those composed of locals from different internationals are called trades councils.

The national or international union is self-governing. Even when affiliated with the AFL–CIO, an international union operates independently and runs its own internal affairs. Obviously, if an affiliated union's policies always run counter to the aims of the AFL–CIO, it might have to withdraw or be expelled. (The Teamsters were expelled in 1957 on charges of domination by corrupt influences and refusal to adopt corrective recommendations. Also expelled at this time, on the same grounds, were the Bakery Workers and the Laundry Workers. The Auto Workers left in 1968 but reaffiliated in 1981.)

Each international is formed by a combination of locals, and in joining the international, a local does forfeit some measure of independence but also gains some measure of support. The amount of control that an international has over its locals varies. No matter what the degree of control, a local must conform to the constitution and regulations of the parent union.

Some subjects generally covered in a union constitution are:

- Conditions under which a local union may be chartered.
- Dues and initiation fees.
- Rules for dealing with employers.
- Procedures for accepting new members.
- Work rules that must be followed.
- Procedures for discipline of members.

Usually, the international has the right to examine the local's financial records and may require regular audit reports.

One method the international can use to control locals is a trusteeship. There were, however, incidents of internationals putting locals into trusteeships for motives less than honorable: a local that objected, for example, to corrupt or incompetent leadership might find itself in trusteeship and its funds taken over by the international. The Landrum-Griffin Act of 1959 regulates trusteeship by requiring reports of such actions and enumerating the reasons for which trusteeships may be established. First, the trusteeship must be established according to the international's constitution and bylaws. The reason for doing so are to correct corruption or financial malpractice, assure the performance of collective bargaining agreements or other duties of a bargaining representative, restore democratic procedures, or carry out "legitimate objects of such labor organization."

An initial report must be filed with the Secretary of Labor and semiannual reports must be submitted thereafter, giving the required information. Penalties can be imposed for violations of the act's provisions on trusteeships.

The functions of an international union include organizing the unorganized in the industry or occupation over which it has jurisdiction, advising and actively assisting locals in contract negotiations, establishing uniform working conditions and pay levels in the industry or occupation, seeing to it that locals live up to the negotiated agreements, and cooperating and participating in AFL–CIO activities if they are affiliates. Just how an international carries out these functions depends on its history and traditions, its leaders, economic and industrial conditions, and to some extent, its size and finances. Most internationals provide a range of expert service to their locals. They do research, especially into complex subjects such as pension plans, provide educational opportunities and training, participate in political and social programs helpful to members, and support desirable legislations. The international is a valuable resource for locals.

The stress the international places on functions varies from time to time. For example when a concentration of unorganized companies appears in one area, the international may decide that it should step up its organizing activities. When it loses members through company closings, layoffs, moves, or changes in technology, it may engage in more aggressive organizing just to stay alive and healthy.

The international takes a more active part in contract negotiations when the negotiation is a first-time effort by a new local, when the bargaining presents unusual difficulty, or when a nationwide company or major industry is involved.

The local union may also feel the international's control when it wants to take strike action. The international's permission may be required, or the strike vote and procedures may have to conform to the international's rules. Strict compliance with these rules is necessary if the local is to receive financial assistance in a strike.

Internationals differ in size. The latest information from the Bureau of Labor Statistics lists the International Association of Siderographers with fifteen members and the Teamsters Union with 1,973,896. The differences in members really gives us a picture of what is happening in our economic and industrial lives. Some trades become obsolete; new occupations are introduced. Some industries contract; others expand.

International unions have presidents, secretary-treasurers, and vice-presidents, but the governing body, the legislative body, the final authority, is the general convention, a representative group composed of delegates from the locals whose number generally is in proportion to the number of paid-up members they represent. In some internationals the number of delegates per paid-up member decreases as the size of the local increases, to avoid domination of the convention by the larger locals. Conventions are very expensive to run; therefore many union constitutions require them only every two or three years, some every five years.

The importance of the convention is sometimes used to illustrate the democratic aspect of unions. Yet, in the past, some unions never held conventions. The officers were elected for life and designated their successors. High-handed administration of some unions and the complete absence of even the appearance of democratic procedures, let alone the procedures, were among the union failings that the Landrum-Griffin Act tried to correct. The act requires every international (and national) to elect officers at least every five years, either by secret ballot or at a convention. In effect this requires conventions to be held every five years or more frequently, since about three quarters of unions elect their officers at a convention.

The convention may be the supreme policy-making body of the international, but day-to-day operations are the responsibility of the general president. The position is one of influence and prestige, although the degree of authority varies from union to union. If his powers are broad, he can issue or revoke charters, appoint or dismiss organizers, issue rulings, interpret the union constitution. Presidents are full-time paid officers, and their pay and perquisites can be extremely generous.

Some internationals also have a full-time paid vice-president, who performs such duties as benefit administration and overseeing organizing activities. In other internationals the vice-presidents are chosen on the basis of a region or branch and hold local office as well. They are paid per diem. The other full-time paid officer usually is a secretary-treasurer.

An international union is run, in most cases, by a general executive council. The board or council usually is composed of the president, secretary-treasurer, and the vice-presidents. The board carries on the business of the union between conventions and functions as the union's constitution dictates.

In addition to elected officers an international has staff members in charge of activities such as research, education, legislation, public relations, and health and safety. The extent of these activities differs from union to union.

One staff activity that all internationals pursue is organizing. The organizers are very important to the union. They may work out of a central location or may be assigned to an area. In some unions the organizers are elected at conventions, but more often they are appointed by the president or the general executive board.

Their major duty is apparent in their title: to organize the unorganized workers in a company, plant, or office. They may do so as part of an over-all organizing campaign in an industry or area. They establish new locals, advise them, interpret the international's policies to them, keep them informed. Since new members are the lifeblood of a union, the organizer's role is especially important.

The chief federation of labor unions now is the AFL–CIO. The current organization evolved out of the older American Federation of Labor (organized in 1886) and the newer Congress of Industrial Organizations (formed in 1935 as the Committee for Industrial Organization). Both organizations merged in 1955. As now constituted, the AFL–CIO has 102 union affiliates (sixty unions are unaffiliated). Its structure is like the old AFL, but it has more authority over the affiliates.

Members of the federation are the national and international unions, state and local labor organizations, trade and industrial departments, and directly affiliated local unions.

As in the international unions, the chief governing body is the convention, held every two years. Each union is entitled to representation according to its membership on which the per capita tax has been paid. Between conventions, the federation is run by its executive officers, the executive council, and the general board. The current top officers are President Lane Kirkland and Secretary-Treasurer Thomas R. Donahue.

The executive council consists of the two top executives and thirty-three vice-presidents, all of whom are presidents of their national or international unions. It meets at least three times a year to carry out its main responsibilities: to propose and evaluate legislation of interest to labor and to safeguard the federation from corrupt or communist influence. The latter responsibility gives the council the right to investigate any affiliate accused of wrong doing and to make recommendations or give directions to the affiliate.

By a two-thirds vote it can suspend a union found guilty on charges of subversion or corruption. Other duties and rights of the council are:

1. To conduct hearings on charges against a council member of malfeasance or maladministration and report on recommended appropriate action to the convention.

2. To remove from office or refuse to seat (by two-thirds vote) any executive officer or council member found to be a member or follower of a subversive organization.

3. To assist unions in organizing activities and charter new national or international unions not in jurisdictional conflict with existing unions.

4. To hear appeals in jurisdictional disputes.

Item number two reflects the turmoil within the labor movement over the issue of communist-dominated or exploited unions during the 1940s and 1950s, while item number four refers to a cause of much labor conflict, jurisdictional disputes.

The general board consists of all thirty-five members of the executive council and a principal member of each affiliated national and international union and department. It meets upon call of the president.

The executive council can establish central bodies on a city, state, or other regional basis, composed of local unions, organizing committees, and directly affiliated local unions. The Department of Labor reported fifty-one state groups (including one for Puerto Rico) and 744 local central bodies in 1979.

Another grouping in the internal structure of the AFL–CIO is by trade and industrial departments. The federation has these departments at present:

> Building trades
> Food trades
> Industrial union
> Maritime trades
> Metal trades
> Public employees
> Railway employees
> Union label

The various national and international unions are also affiliated with departments appropriate to their own activites. For example the International Brotherhood of Boilermakers, Iron Ship Builders, Blacksmiths, Forgers and Helpers belongs to several of the above departments. Each department also holds a convention.

The AFL–CIO is the largest and best-known labor federation, but three others that deserve mention are noted by the U.S. Department of Labor. One is the Assembly of Governmental Employees (AGE) which was founded in 1952 as the National Conference of

Independent Public Employee Associations. It is composed of forty-eight state, county, and local affiliated organizations. The second is the National Federation of Independent Unions (NFIU), and the third is the Telecommunications International Union.

The latest available information from the Labor Department gave 102 unions as the number affiliated with the AFL–CIO. In addition there were sixty-four unions with no affiliations. Besides organizations classified as unions by the Labor Department, there were thirty-two professional and state employee associations. The department, adding up the affiliated and the unaffiliated, the unions and the associations, reported membership of 24.4 million in 1978. The data recorded are out of date almost as soon as printed, since labor unions gain or lose members fairly frequently. Moreover, the data are dependent upon the unions' supplying information promptly and completely; this is not always feasible. But the figures do give a generally accurate picture of the organized labor movement.

The various activities carried on at all levels of the union structure require money. How much money the local or the international has on hand depends on what services or functions it is carrying on. During a strike, for instance, the loss of dues and the expenditure of strike funds may drain the treasury. If a union dispenses benefits, the amounts disbursed vary from time to time.

A union is an organization; it has administrative expenses: office space, utilities, clerical help, accounting, legal services, and organizing expenses. Officers' salaries and traveling expenses must be paid. At the international level these expenses are increased by special needs: economists to prepare negotiation material, extra lawyers if litigation is under way, benefit specialists for proper administration of union benefit or welfare funds, accountants, public relations experts. Whether the union's emphasis on functions or services is at the local or the international level affects finances too. The salaries of the international officers and their expenses often are on a par with what top company executives receive. In other cases the general president receives only slightly more than an ordinary union member. The full-time secretary-treasurer and the vice-presidents must be paid accordingly. And, of course, staff must be compensated adequately.

The basic source of union funds is payment of dues to the local union. Dues usually are paid on a monthly basis. Beside dues, there are initiation fees, assessments, and reinstatement fees (fines may also be collected). The local collects from its members, or if a checkoff arrangement exists, dues are forwarded by the employer to the local. Then the locals forward specified sums to the international union and to any state or local organization with which they are affiliated. The international pays a per capita sum to the AFL–CIO.

Some unions used to charge exorbitant initiation fees so as to limit the number of workers in a trade, and some unions used to levy assessments rather freely. The Labor Management Relations Act makes it an unfair labor practice for the unions to charge an initiation fee that the National Labor Relations Board finds "excessive or discriminatory under the circumstances." The National Labor Relations Board is given the power to decide, taking into consideration the practices and customs of unions in the industry and the pay of employees.

The Landrum-Griffin Act provides that members of a union must, by majority vote, decide whether dues are to be increased or initiation fees raised.

An important function of the AFL–CIO is the resolution of jurisdictional disputes among its affiliates. By jurisdiction is meant:

> . . . *the authority claimed by a union to represent certain groups of workers either in a specific type of work or occupation in a particular industry or industries or in a certain geographic area. The claim of jurisdiction may come from a grant, by AFL–CIO, of a charter giving a union the right to*

organize employees in a particular area, both as to work or industry. . . .

Union jurisdiction or claim of jurisdiction will vary over a period of time as the changes in industrial technology lead to the use of new materials, new machinery, and new facilities, so that the union itself must take cognizance of these changes and seek to maintain membership in that particular area of production or extend to other areas should employment decline within its own previous jurisdiction. (Harold S. Roberts, *Dictionary of Industrial Relations*)

Jurisdictional disputes occurred more in the original AFL unions than in the CIO's early affiliates. The Labor Management Relations Act makes it an unfair labor practice for a union to strike to force or require an employer "to assign particular work to employees in a particular labor organization or in a particular trade, craft, or class rather than to employees in another labor organizations or in another trade, craft, or class" unless the employer is not comforming to a National Labor Relations Board certification of the proper bargaining representative.

If the conflicting unions cannot resolve their differences, the board can make the decision. As a practical matter, however, the AFL–CIO decides these questions. The constitution of the federation provides the machinery for dealing with jurisdictional problems. Since the inception of its Internal Disputes Plan in 1962, about two thousand cases were filed. The 1979 report of the AFL–CIO Executive Council stated that fifty-six percent of its complaints were settled by mediation; the remainder were to be decided by an impartial umpire. In only twenty-five cases had a union failed to comply with the decisions; sanctions were imposed by the executive council and compliance was eventually reached in eleven of those cases.

Changes in or extensions of jurisdiction are crucial in times of rapid change. Some unions take in just about any members they can. The United Mine Workers (Ind.) have long had a catch-all District 50, which includes members outside the coal mining industry. District 65 of the Distributive Workers (Ind.) ranged far and wide in its organizing activities. In 1979 the Distributive Workers merged with the United Automobile Workers, now back in the federation fold.

Mergers may be a means of eliminating conflict and strengthening efficiency, but they also are a method of survival and sometimes result in incongruous combinations. For example the Tobacco Workers joined with the Bakery Workers to form the Bakery, Confectionary and Tobacco Workers International Union (AFL–CIO). Another merger that reflects change in the industry is that of the United Shoe Workers with the Amalgamated Clothing and Textile Workers (AFL–CIO), a union born of an earlier merger.

Unusual combinations of workers and industries in the current group of international unions are the result of the unions' need to survive. Conglomerates exist now in the union world as well as the industrial world.

CHAPTER 8

What Union Membership Means

Joining a union is not the same as joining a social club, a political organization, or a professional association. Getting in, if your occupation, company, institution, or agency is unionized, may not be difficult. In fact you may have no choice but to join. Getting out also is different from a resignation from a club.

One of the most persuasive reasons for joining a union is to keep a job. When the labor agreement between employer and union contains a union shop clause, all workers covered by the agreement *must* become union members within a specified period of time after the contract goes into effect (if it is a new agreement) or after they are hired. The legal minimum is thirty days, but the period of time can be longer.

The contract provision under which a person must be a union member before hiring is called a closed shop. The closed shop was banned by the Labor–Management Relations Act of 1947 (the Taft-Hartley Act). A later amendment to that law, however, permits what amounts to a closed shop in the building construction industry. In states with right-to-work laws both the closed shop and the union shop are forbidden. The union shop is legal in about sixty percent of the states; these states are those in the northeastern United States, in the heavily industrialized middle west, and the state of California.

Holding onto a job is a concern for most working people so this reason for union membership is a compelling one. Other reasons are for job security, for protection against unfair discipline or an unwarranted discharge.

In a non-union company an employee can be fired at will or at whim. The employer does not have to give a good reason for the discharge; in fact no reason is necessary. Unless the discharge may be found to be a violation of a law, for example, an anti-discrimination statute, the discharged employee says out. Since loss of a job is the industrial equivalent of capital punishment, especially when jobs are hard to find, the possibility of an unjustified discharge is an unsettling fact.

When a company is unionized, protection does exist. Union contracts do not forbid discharge; what they do is stipulate that ''just cause'' must exist. Some contracts even specify the offenses for which an employee can be discharged. Some attach or incorporate lists of regulations and state the disciplinary penalties, up to and including discharge, for various violations of company rules.

What is significant is that the employee, through the grievance procedure, can challenge the justification for the discipline or the discharge. The union usually takes over and processes the grievance, acting like a defense attorney. The employer must prove that ''just cause'' existed, that the employee did commit the offense, and that the penalty, if warranted, is consistent with company practice.

Protection from unfair discipline or discharge is only one aspect of job security. Another, which has particular importance in times of economic distress, is protection against an unfair layoff. No one would dispute a company's need to lay off employees when work is not available, when inventories have piled up and customers have vanished, when a plant or department must be shut down for repairs or for the installation of new equipment. The right to determine production needs and the size and composition of the work crew frequently is set forth in the labor agreement as a "management prerogative." But if the choice of the individual employees to be laid off is entirely up to management, it is possible that favoritism or bias would affect their selection, and this happens often enough when a non-union company has a reduction in force.

Unions stress seniority, the right to a job based on how long a person has been employed in a plant, department, occupation, or the company as a whole. (The actual kind of seniority that applies in a situation is determined by contract.) When a unionized company has a layoff, a method based on seniority governs the order in which men and women leave their jobs. The usual method is last hired, first out. This means that the senior employees have the greatest amount of job security.

Some authorities point out that seniority is a relative right; the worker exercises his seniority for various purposes—layoff, for example—in relation to the rights of other employees. But the right to fair treatment is absolute, comparable to the constitutional right to due process of law. Under our laws a man is presumed innocent until proven guilty.

Two of the main reasons for joining a union are getting a job and keeping it. Another reason is protection from the employer's arbitrary or capricious actions. In addition to discipline and discharge include these changes in hours, meal periods or rest breaks, holidays, vacations, benefit plans, and just about any working condition.

For an example, take the coffee break, a time-honored custom in many companies. In one department everyone takes about fifteen minutes between 9:30 and 10:30 in the morning for a cup of coffee or tea. In comes a new supervisor eager to improve production. On his pocket calculator he finds that twenty-five people taking fifteen minutes per day, five days a week results in a loss of 31.5 hours, almost a full work week; he sends forth a decree: no time out for morning coffee. If you must, bring it into the office and drink it before 9:00 A.M. when the work day starts.

Union members would probably file a grievance that the new supervisor, disregarding past practice, had arbitrarily abolished the coffee break. They might or might not win the grievance, but they would have had the chance to voice a protest, and management would have been obliged to sit down and talk with the union.

This may seem a trivial example, but it serves to illustrate the point that once a labor organization represents employees, a company or members of its managerial or supervising staff, cannot take unilateral action on wages or conditions of work without negotiating with the union. A whole array of court decisions since the passage of the National Labor Relations Act in 1935 has brought us to the point where companies are obliged to bargain collectively, to negotiate with their unions about almost every matter affecting employment. For instance consider the case of a company that pays all the costs of a health insurance program. The company decides that it will expand the plan to provide more liberal benefits. Does it have to bargain with the union? Of course. Health insurance is a negotiable item. Perhaps the union members do not want more generous benefits but would prefer a higher wage increase or a better pension plan.

Another reason for joining a union is a social one. Joining the same one as your co-workers provides an identification with a group. Unions usually provide a variety of social as well as business activities that give members and their families an opportunity to enjoy or educate themselves, all activities reinforcing the identification with the labor organization. Pressure from peers in the work group may draw a person into the union; pleasurable activities may make the association worthwhile on social as well as economic grounds. Moreover, many union members are relatives of other union members. They have grown up in households where union membership is matter-of-fact and accepted.

Many working people also like to believe that they can play

some part in shaping what happens to them on the job. Work, after all, is central to the lives of most people; it gives us purpose, importance; it is a kind of framework or support. Yet in all phases of our lives we have become numbers, nameless people whom a computer recognizes only by a Social Security number, a health insurance number, a credit card number, a payroll number. At work our fates are determined by the top executives, who make policy, by the middle managers who, employees themselves, must implement policy. It is a rare company, indeed, where what happens to the employees at the bottom of the structure and how they react is communicated to the top. This feeling of helplessness before the whole machinery of the organization can propel individuals into unions. Through collective bargaining, at least, the desires and needs of employees can be articulated.

The local union, the foundation of the entire union structure, is intended to give its individual members a voice in deciding what happens to them on the job.

That same local union also offers some union members the scope to demonstrate and use abilities which the job does not. Leadership ability and management skills can be exercised within the union; effective union leaders like effective managers, must possess these qualities. So the union provides an opportunity for men and women to utilize qualifications that their jobs do not require and to advance to positions of leadership not available to them in the organization. Almost all top union officials rise from within the ranks; they are not brought in as executive trainees and put on a fast track to the top.

Finally, some people are committed to the labor movement. They believe that only through strong unions can working men and women exercise any power at all and achieve their aspirations. Many early unionists and union leaders were dedicated to the ideals of a labor movement.

Take some of the reasons that propel people into unions, turn them around, and you will have reasons why some individuals do not join unions. Peer pressure is one. Just as wanting to be part of the group influences some persons into joining a union, pressure of a different sort helps people out. If a worker's colleagues are anti-union, a person may not want to buck them and come out for a union.

Social status, family background, and education also play a part. Many white collar and professional workers see themselves as moving into executive positions; executives are not union members. Or, some associate unions with blue collar workers and people on the lower rungs of the social ladder. Joining a union is socially unacceptable. That some of the highest paid people in any occupation—actors, newspapermen, television personalities—are union members does not occur to them. (Ronald Reagan was once the head of a union, the Screen Actors Guild.)

Family background enters into one's perceptions of unions. If no one in the family ever was a union member, the notion of union membership seems foreign. Conversely, if one's father, mother, or other relative was a union member, an active one or an officer, union membership is accepted as a matter of fact. Similarly, until recently, our educational system largely ignored the labor movement. History courses, even in secondary schools and colleges, gave little if any, attention to labor unions. Only in the last twenty years have teachers been unionized to any extent; children in elementary schools as well as in college now know that an educated professional may be a union member too.

Some people are independent souls. The idea of giving up a portion of their freedom by joining other workers in a concerted activity, such as a union, frequently is distasteful to them. They believe that they can strike a better bargain on their own: their work experience may bear this out. People who have had a comparatively smooth time in establishing their careers without union assistance are not likely to feel they need a third party to act for them in a work situation.

To others the cost of union membership may seem too high in view of the benefits achieved and the loss of individual freedom. Union members pay initiation fees, dues, and from time to time special assessments; the returns may seem insufficient.

No doubt, too, the unsavory reputation of certain union leaders and the autocratic, even violent, practices of some unions put off others who would be prospects for union membership. Paying dues to a local allegedly or actually connected with organized crime is not an appealing or encouraging thought.

There is no doubt that the crime and corruption that have been disclosed within the labor movement are cogent reasons for some people to avoid any association with unions. Incidents of violence, also typical of some unions, are not conducive to faith in unions.

Finally, many persons do not become union members because the opportunity does not arise. They may work in an area or industry where the labor movement is not strong, or in a company too small to be worth the effort and expense of a union's organizing drive, or in a company that does not supply sufficient reasons for employees to seek or welcome organization.

A person who wishes to join a union cannot just choose one that looks attractive and send in his application for membership, nor can he look around for friends who are members and ask a couple of them to put him up for membership. A group of workers, however, can approach a union and ask to be organized.

Every union has its own regulations about acceptance, retention, and loss of membership. Even union rules, however, must conform to the law. The Labor–Management Relations Act specifically gives a union the right "to prescribe its own rules with respect to the acquisition or retention of membership." This same law also makes it an unfair labor practice—a violation of the law—for an employer to discriminate against any employee for nonmembership in a union if the employer believes that membership was not available to the employee on the same terms and conditions applicable to other members, or if the employer believes that membership was denied or terminated for a reason other than the employee's failure to pay his dues or the initiation fees.

So the union's right to establish its own membership rules is a qualified one under the law. This right is further qualified by the civil rights legislation, which is applicable to unions as well as employers.

In the past some unions did discriminate on the basis of age, sex, color, race, religion, or national origin. Some required members to be citizens. Although the constitution of the international union may have been nondiscriminatory, what a local union did to circumvent the international usually was disregarded. Some unions that did admit black members had separate all-black locals and signed labor agreements permitting separate seniority lists for black workers. Other unions (the carpenters, for example) were father-and-son unions; an individual was admitted to apprenticeship or membership only if his father was a union member. All others, blacks and women, in particular, were kept out. In some unions a person must be in the craft itself in order to be a union member; since few women were in these crafts, they were shut out completely.

The Civil Rights Act of 1964, Title VII, the Equal Employment Opportunity Act, had a significant impact on unions, since they too may not discriminate on grounds of race, color, sex, religion, or national origin.

Having said what unions cannot do, let us see what they can do to regulate membership. In the crafts or trades, where a lengthy period of training is necessary, union rules cover apprentices. To protect the jobs of full-fledged journeymen members and to maintain a satisfactory level of skills, unions control the number of apprentices they admit (both men and women now) and prescribe the education and training for them. The wage rates for apprentices usually are set at a percentage of the journeymen's rates. The rules for acceptance may require an aptitude test, set minimum and maximum age limits, specify the ratio of apprentices to journeymen in a shop, and detail the length of the training period. Additional conditions may be specified as well. In some cases apprentices join the union as soon as they are accepted; in others they are not permitted to join until they become journeymen.

The apprenticeship route is one way to become a union member in a skilled trade or a craft, such as electrician or operating engineer. The other main road to union membership is employment in the trade or industry over which the union has jurisdiction.

The actual acceptance of members and the review of their qualifications are up to the locals. Sometimes a union grants honorary membership to people who never have worked in the trade, a prominent person, for instance. Union staff members and even some officers who may not have worked in the trade or industry may be permitted to become members. This would be most unusual, however, as most unions have a requirement that officers and staff must have trade experience.

Generally, the names of candidates for membership are presented at a meeting of the local for approval by a majority—a number determined by the local's rules. In a few cases unions allow rejection of a candidate if a small number of votes are cast against him. In practice most unions make acceptance easy.

What happens if an individual is rejected? The name may be presented at several successive meetings. If a person is rejected by one local, most internationals state that he cannot be accepted by another in a given period of time without the consent of the first local. An appeal to the general executive board of the international also is possible. Again, the reasons for rejection cannot be for any reason that the law would consider discriminatory. For example it is common practice for a union constitution to state that a candidate for membership must be "of good moral character." If evidence indicated that an individual's "good moral character" was nonexistent, he probably could be rejected. Some unions require the prospective member to be qualified and to be endorsed by several older members. The union may investigate the applicant's competence and turn him down if it decides he is unqualified. (The older members who sponsored him may be fined if they knew he was not competent.) This concern over a candidate's competency applies more in the skilled trades and in unions which supply workers for employers (as in the building construction trades) than in the industrial unions that encompass all types of workers.

Once in a union, can a member resign? You can transfer, retire, withdraw honorably, or you can be suspended or expelled. "Resign" doesn't apply.

A union member can be suspended for failing to pay dues and assessments for the period of time specified by the union. If the individual who fails to pay his dues is working under a union shop contract, he can be fired.

Expulsion is a serious matter and is, therefore, pretty much confined to serious causes. The expulsion procedure, since it can also involve loss of a job, is surrounded by safeguards. Each union has its own procedure, but the Landrum-Griffin Act of 1959 (Labor Management Reporting and Disclosure Act), which amended the Labor–Management Relations Act, specifically provides:

No member of any labor organization may be fined, suspended, expelled, or otherwise disciplined except for nonpayment of dues by such organization or by any officer thereof unless such member has been a) served with written specific charges; b) given a reasonable time to prepare his defense; c) afforded a full and fair hearing.

In a way the law provides the union member with due process so far as the union is concerned, just as the grievance procedure gives him due process so far as the employer is concerned.

What would a union consider grounds for suspension or expulsion? Generally, "conduct unbecoming a union member," "violation of union rules," or a related cause. In the past these frequently were stretched to include criticism of incumbent officers, opposition to union policies and the like, making it extremely difficult or impossible for a member who simply wanted to express dissatisfaction or to work for change within the union. Some unions solved the problem by simply scotching all opposition by any means available, including violence. The issue of freedom of speech and assembly for union members is dealt with by the Landrum-Griffin Act. Title I of the act, called the Bill of Rights for Union Members, reads:

> *Every member of any labor organization shall have the right to meet and assemble freely with other members; and to express any views, arguments, or opinions; and to express at meetings of the labor organization his views, upon candidates in an election of the labor organization or upon any business properly before the meeting, subject to the organization's established and reasonable rules pertaining to the conduct of meetings:* Provided *that nothing herein shall be construed to impair the right of a labor organization to adopt and enforce reasonable rules as to the responsibility of every member toward the organization as an institution and to his refraining from conduct that would interfere with the performance of its legal and contractual obligations.*

Thus a member who took part in a wildcat strike in violation of contract could be disciplined according to the union's rules and, perhaps, be suspended or expelled. But a disgruntled member who goes about complainng and being a nuisance may have to be endured.

Suspended members can regain their good standing. If the suspension was for nonpayment of dues and fees, reinstatement usually requires payment in full of all back amounts that are due. Some unions also require payment of a reinstatement fee, which may be higher, lower or the same as the original initiation fee. The idea is that the fee should serve as deterrent to members who are inclined to be delinquent in their obligations. Of course when the labor agreement with the employer contains a checkoff clause, unions do not have to worry about nonpayment of dues. The sums are deducted from the pay of each union member and forwarded to the union.

Unions provide for situations in which a worker moves from one area to another but stays in the occupation or industry over which the international union has jurisdiction. A member can transfer from one local to another. But, if the new local has unemployed members, it may refuse transfers. Some internationals require their locals to accept transfers, especially those of long-time members. Unions may also permit "courtesy privileges" for a member who is on a temporary or special job. Craft unions occasionally issue "traveling cards" that allow a member to take a job elsewhere for a limited time, without applying for a transfer. The member must then register with the local union that has jurisdiction over the job and pay dues to it. A permanent transfer may require a "clearance card" indicating that the individual holding it is a member in good standing of the local from which he is transferring. If the new local has higher initiation fees than the old local, the transferee may have to pay the difference—it depends upon the union rules.

Members who are out of work or off on extended leaves present different problems. Some unions reduce their dues for unemployed members; others allow the unemployed members to be in arrears for a period of time much longer than would be tolerated for working members. This is true when the dues affect the individual's pension or other benefits. A third variation is for the union to wipe out the dues obligation when a member is laid off, on strike, or ill for an extended period. What happens always depends on the union's own rules. Union members who are on military service may be free of all requirements for paying dues until a specified time after their return from military duty (naturally, this does not apply to a member on a short leave for training).

It may happen that a union member changes his work completely, leaving his job and the industry. Or a member may retire. Those whose new jobs are outside the union's jurisdiction may get withdrawal cards; in this way, they can return to their original union if circumstances change. Members who retire also withdraw honorably, with a retirement or honorary membership card.

Managerial and supervisory personnel may belong to a union, but they are specifically excluded from the protection of the Labor–Management Relations Act. Thus the law offers neither encouragement nor safeguards for any collective bargaining activities by them. Consequently, with the exception of some craft unions, you will find that virtually no union in the private industrial sector has members who are supervisors. The definition of ''supervisor'' under the law is:

> . . . *any individual having authority, in the interest of the employer, to hire, transfer, suspend, lay off, recall, promote, discharge, assign, reward, or discipline other employees, or responsibly to direct them, or to adjust their grievances, or effectively to recommend such action, or if in connection with the foregoing the exercise of such authority is not of a merely routine or clerical nature, but requires the use of independent judgment.*

Although all supervisory personnel are excluded from coverage of the law, all professional employees are not. Professional employees who are neither supervisors nor managers are entitled to the protection of the Labor–Management Relations Act in their bargaining activities. But whether an individual is a nonmanagerial professional often depends upon interpretation of the law. For example the U.S. Supreme Court ruled that professors in private colleges are managerial as well as professional and so not entitled to collective bargaining rights under the LMRA.

What about rank-and-file members who become supervisors? They may not wish to lose any benefits built up during their union membership and may wish to be reinstated in the union if necessary. In these cases some unions provide them with honorary membership cards. As honorary members they no longer participate in union activities but they can retain their benefits and, should their circumstances change, be reinstated to active membership.

CHAPTER 9

What Does a Union Do?

Those whose knowledge about unions is derived solely from newspaper headlines or brief items on television and radio news round-ups tend to associate unions only with strikes or even violence. They also tend to associate union officials only with illegal activities, with embezzlement or extortion, with corruption, with ties to organized crime.

Strikes, violence, criminal behavior: all are aspects of the labor movement. Strikes, however, may be legal work stoppages; "concerted activity" of certain kinds is protected by law. Violence may be initiated by the union; it also can be provoked deliberately by anti-union forces, although some union officials are in jail and others should be, thousands more are honest men and women working for the benefit of their organizations and their members. Unions are no better and no worse than the rest of our society.

Union activities cover a surprising range. Collective bargaining, however, is a primary activity. Negotiating the first labor agreement between employer and union or negotiating renewals is of prime importance. But before a contract can be negotiated, some structure or framework—a local union—must exist. A local is made up of individual members.

The first concern of a labor union is getting members, organizing the unorganized. Every national union carries on organizing activities through a staff of professional organizers. These days the organizers are likely to be well-educated, sophisticated individuals, with a college degree. Although their carefully planned organizing efforts will be aided by rank-and-file members, union organizers must have the same knowledge of human motivation and skill in communications techniques as any vice-president of marketing. Organizers in a sense are marketing people, marketing the concept of union membership.

Organizers have to be good at their jobs. Most companies and institutions do not put out welcome mats for unions, nor do they cower behind the office door or plant gate, waiting for the union to attack and conquer. Companies vulnerable to unionization often have consultants on retainer or experts on staff to forestall or defeat attempts to organize them. If this sounds like warfare, it often is.

Unionization of a company can come about in several ways. One way is an all-out drive by a national union or several unions in a promising locality. With the spread of industrialization to rural areas, a concentration of prospects for unionization exists where once only a few farmhands could be seen. In the United States unions have begun to look to the Sun Belt, in particular Texas, where new industries have settled in and where older industries have expanded. Some companies that left the industrialized and unionized cities of the Northeast for the wide-open, union-free areas of the Southwest will soon confront the kinds of labor situations they thought they left behind.

This is simply a repetition of an old union pattern: Go where the numbers are and organize the unorganized.

Unions also will aim at the non-union companies in an industry that already is heavily unionized. If the union can show the non-union workers that they lag behind their organized colleagues in pay and benefits it may convince them to join up. Unions want to standardize wages and benefits within an industry.

Occasionally, workers will invite a union to come in and organize, especially if they are deeply dissatisfied about their wages or working conditions. When this happens, the union gains the advantage of a ripe-for-organization group with inside knowledge of the company, knowledge the union can utilize in dealing with the employer.

When a multi-plant company already is unionized in a few locations, it may be possible for a union to organize at a newly opened facility. In these cases the company is less likely to resist unionization actively or effectively. Again, the union has intimate knowledge about the company and its policies.

Union efforts to organize may extend over a period of years. Sometimes one union is successful after others have failed arriving on the scene just when a combination of events, such as changes in the composition of the work force or in management, makes organization possible.

Whatever the avenue of approach, the union goal is organization, which is essential to union health. If a union merely sits back, content with the membership it has, with the advances it has made, it will die. Members retire, die, leave the industry or the company. Companies go out of business, move; technology changes; markets evaporate or alter; customers and clients change. Unless a union is alert, flexible, and able to expand, even to merge with another, it can, like a company, go bankrupt.

The signing of a contract does not mean that both parties to it will abide by its letter or spirit. The union ordinarily is more zealous than the employer in policing the contract. The employer signs, but the actual terms of the contract are implemented by many levels of management, down to the first-line supervisor. Usually, company personnel are not so well versed in the meaning of the contract as are union leaders. Most unions make quite an effort to train their union stewards in policies and intensive procedures; company efforts may not be so comprehensive. Inadvertent as well as deliberate violations of contract provisions occur. The union stewards, if well trained and vigilant, are quick to spot any possible contract violations. (Companies will say stewards are too hasty and often see a violation where none exists.) Once the contract has been signed, the local union, through its officers and stewards, is concerned with seeing that its terms are carried out.

If terms of a contract are violated, either in regard to an individual worker or a group of workers, the union can seek redress through the grievance procedure. Handling grievances is an important union activity. In a non-union company an employee certainly can have a gripe or a grievance, but in most cases he cannot do much about it. It is the rare non-union company that has a satisfactory—to the employee—grievance procedure. The procedure, after all, exists at the pleasure of the company, which can amend or halt it whenever it wishes. Even if the employee has the support of a company ombudsman, who is supposed to be impartial, the employee has no recourse if his grievance or complaint is found to be without merit. And he may have the nagging feeling that impartiality is not possible in the situation.

In a unionized company the grievance procedure is part of the contract. An employee with a grievance has the support of his union in seeking a remedy. His union steward usually is his first avenue of approach, the person who deals with the company supervisor. Should the grievance be taken to higher levels, both in the company and the union, the union backing will continue, right up and through the arbitration procedure, if necessary.

Must a union take up a grievance? Generally, it must. If it refuses to handle a grievance for a union member, it may be in violation of the law. Now some people do bring up frivolous or ridiculous grievances. The experienced union steward often can talk the individual out of pursuing the matter further; on the other hand the steward may process the grievance, knowing it will be turned down at some stage of the grievance procedure. A grievance can be resolved at any stage of the procedure; frequently a knowledgeable union steward and an equally knowledgeable supervisor settle most grievances between themselves. Ordinarily only the gravest grievances go the full route, including an arbitration hearing, a discharge grievance, for example, or a grievance over a significant interpretation of a contract clause.

The processing of grievances according to the provisions of the contract is day-to-day collective bargaining. It is a time-consuming activity for the union, second only to contract negotiation in importance. Again, most unions provide excellent training for the stewards, who are the employees' first recourse when they have a complaint. Grievance procedures are time consuming for the company, too, but they give both parties to the agreement an orderly method for resolving differences and for seeing why and where conflicts arise. (Under some contracts the company also can initiate grievances.) Both union and employer can use the grievance procedure in a constructive way: the records can be a basis for seeking changes in subsequent negotiations of the contract provisions that need clarification or change.

Another area in which most unions now show more interest than they used to is health and safety on the job. A few unions, the United Mine Workers in particular, have always been concerned with worker safety, and have lobbied successfully for legislation to protect workers. John L. Lewis, President of the United Mine Workers, was tireless in his efforts to gain both safety legislation to reduce the hazards in mining and compensation and care for miners who were the victims of occupational accidents and disease. Lewis had been a miner, had seen death in the mines, and had watched his own father suffer from the dread "black lung" disease, silicosis.

A disaster that horrified the public and drew attention to the unsafe working conditions of factory workers occurred in New York City on March 25, 1911. This was a fire at the Triangle Shirtwaist Company that killed about one hundred fifty employees, most of them young women. Those whom fire and smoke did not kill lost their lives jumping from the eighth floor. Doors to exits had been bolted shut, the newspapers reported, to keep employees from pilfering goods. The tragedy gave momentum to the union movement in the garment trades and resulted in the appointment of a Factory Investigating Committee by the New York State Legislature.

This union, the International Ladies' Garment Workers Union, is another that from its inception fought to improve working conditions, shorten working hours, and raise wages. The sweatshop conditions in the women's clothing industry were notorious. Naturally long hours of work in unventilated, crowded rooms, the well and the ill side-by-side, spread disease. Tuberculosis was the price paid by many workers.

At first the International Ladies' Garment Workers Union looked to the state for help. But after the general strike of 1911 in New York the union changed directions. From both union and employers came the notion of having a Joint Board of Sanitary Control. The board listed the problems as inadequate protection against fire; dirty floors, ceiling, walls, water closets; defective plumbing; lack of sufficient water closets and rubbish receptacles; lack of ventilation; air pollution (because of the use of coal and gas irons); and inadequate lighting. Standards were set and enforcement provided, although the board had no legal status or police power. It entered premises only with the consent of the owners or shop chairman and relied upon persuasion, counsel, and where appropriate, the state labor department and the city health department. Where these measures failed, a ''Sanitary Strike'' resulted.

What is of interest to us now in this brief account of a union's early effort to provide its members with a safe working environment is this: Sweatshops are still with us. Every now and again they are heard of, usually in connection with exploitation of immigrant labor, people who are ignorant of their legal rights and fearful of losing a job. Another reason for singling out the International

Ladies' Garment Workers Union: it is one of the first examples of joint employer-union efforts in health and safety. In some companies union and management representatives comprise a committee which tries to inculcate safe work habits and to eliminate hazardous working conditions. As more knowledge about the dangers inherent in materials and methods of work and the disposal of waste becomes known to all of us—including union members—even those unions that were not in the forefront of safety movements have had to become concerned.

Unions in the United States generally hailed the Occupational Health and Safety Act of 1970 but in the years following its enactment shared the disappointment with its implementation. Among the causes for dissatisfacton were the lengthy and all but unintelligible standards, the excessive cost of meeting them, and the insufficient number of government inspections to enforce the act. With the agency's funds cut even more in a political climate unsympathetic to the Occupational Health and Safety Act, it will be up to the labor movement to take the initiative. Evidence of this growing activity among unions is shown by the contract provisions regarding worker health and safety: the joint committees, the training of union personnel as health and safety experts, the funds for the study of industry conditions and worker health funds sometimes provided by the industry itself—as in steel.

State laws on worker health and safety range from the conprehensive and up-to-date to the totally inadequate. One area of statutory protection does exist in every state is Workers' Compensation, the system of compensation for job-connected injury, disease, or death. The provisions vary from one state to another; unions favor and lobby for laws more liberal for workers and more severe on employers.

Although the international labor unions do not, as in Europe, constitute a labor party, they are politically active. Unions are concerned with influencing the election of federal and state officials who will support the labor cause through favorable legislation. The Taft-Hartley Act makes it illegal for a union to contribute funds toward financing campaigns for national office. Union members, of course, can contribute as individuals, but unions can and do use their funds to educate their members. Union newspapers give the voting records of candidates office and state the union's views.

For their part candidates court the unions. That a national union will endorse one or the other office seeker is important, even though union members do not vote as a block. It would be a rare candidate who spurned the support of any major union; the candidate (federal or state) who is invited to speak at an AFL–CIO convention or the convention of any major union and who gets an enthusiastic reception deems himself fortunate.

Besides trying to elect its friends labor also tries to influence legislation, so a major union activity is lobbying. At the national level the AFL–CIO and the national unions seek to get the kind of legislation that benefits labor and to block legislation that labor considers harmful. The same kind of lobbying is carried on at state and local levels by statewide union bodies or by state, county, and local bodies representing different trades or industries.

Labor's legislative interests are broader than those concerned only with union affairs and union members. Some unions (the International Ladies' Garment Workers Union, for one) have long been interested in social legislation, laws affecting the quality of life for union and non-union workers, for example, Social Security, health insurance, housing, civil rights, environmental protection, consumer safeguards, and the like. As the public—including union members—becomes both more informed and vocal about these issues, even those unions that never cared about legislation unless it directly affected them may have to take a stand.

Unions have had additional concerns about their members, concerns reflected in contract negotiations. Many early unions, for instance, provided death and burial benefits, and looked out for the widows and orphans. Before the Social Security system was established a few unions had established their own pension plans or negotiated plans. Even basic health care was provided by some labor organizations.

However, unions also provide a whole range of activities encompassing the interests and needs of all kinds of members: young and old, the culture-minded and the sports-minded, the families and the singles. Unions may provide these activities and services not only for the American workers but also for the recent immigrants in the native languages of those immigrants.

One way to illustrate the scope of these activities is to list some recently offered by Local 23-25 of the International Ladies' Garment Workers Union:

I   Classes in or for

English
Citizenship
Sewing machine operation
Sewing machine repairs
Senior citizens
Knitting
Pattern making
Textile painting
Spanish
Preretirement

Budget
Oil painting
Political education
First aid
Chorus singing
Disco dancing
Physical fitness
Nutrition guidance
Meditation
Bowling

II   Services

Lending library
Voters' registration
Unemployment insurance
Personal problems
Alcoholism clinic
Food stamps
Drugs and medicines

Consumer problems
Housing problems
Immigration classes
Social security
Blood bank
Diet and weight control
Medicaid

The local also had trips available, from a tour of the New York City museums to a tour of the People's Republic of China. Several points are worth noting: Although this local is in New York City, where many of these activities are readily available through other sources, the union offers them and finds members take advantage of them. Attending classes or participating in activities with other union members builds a bond of fellowship. The announcement of these activities is made in three languages, English, Spanish, and Chinese. Many of the courses offered are aimed at immigrants, at the newest arrivals in the industrial world, the classes in citizenship, for example, the help with food stamps, immigration, and housing problems. The union's activities offer up-to-date information on nutrition and consumer problems.

The program of Local 23-25 is cited merely as an example of the educational and social programs for members. Not all locals or nationals provide so many activities, but the ones that do give their members opportunities to get together or that provide information to help cope with daily problems are less likely to have apathetic membership. The list of local activites proves that education is a major union activity, particularly education of members about economics and political conditions as the union sees them and education about the union itself. Educational activities are carried on in a variety of ways: labor newspapers and periodicals, pamphlets, audiovisual materials, radio and television. The International Ladies' Garment Workers Union, for example, had card ads in the New York City subways and on buses stressing union-made garments.

The materials for education are frequently presented in the native language of the worker. Even when a union paper is in English, it may have a page or two of important news translated into a foreign tongue—Spanish, for example.

Variety is the key to subject matter. Some craft journal papers contain information of a technical nature, such as new materials and new methods. Local publications contain personal news as well as articles on the latest contract settlements. No subject seems to be neglected, from recipes to items of interest to retirees. All material, naturally, is written from the union's point of view.

Union efforts in the public relations field are relatively new and not especially productive as yet. Very few people who are not union members or who have no professional concern with unions know much about them. The general public tends to rely upon personal prejudice or misinformation.

Some labor unions make positive attempts to provide information, for example, sending speakers to clubs, associations, or other groups. One effective method of public relations has been cooperation in community affairs, with fund-raising activities for local charities, with support for local groups or the elderly, with attempting to keep a hospital or institution open.

In strike situations some unions have taken the same route as employers, using advertisements in local papers to explain their positions or appearing on local radio seeking housing for low-income families or for television. Public relations, however, remains an activity that unions do not, as yet, engage in with marked success.

CHAPTER 10

What's in a Contract?

The aim of contract negotiations is achievement of an agreement between union and employer covering the wages and working conditions of employees. The employees, who have the most to gain or lose under the contract, are not parties to it; the union represents them and the union officers sign for them. In fact, as purists point out, a union agreement really is not a contract. But we call it a contract; we talk of abiding by the contract and violating the contract, and the contract is enforceable at law.

Contracts come in all sizes and variations. Some are very short, giving only the essential provisions such as wage rates. Others are lengthy and detailed. In some instances, where the parties have had contractual relations for a number of years, the original contract stays in effect; all that the parties do, after negotiating a renewal, is to enumerate any changes in a memorandum of understanding.

Although contracts differ from union to union and from industry to industry, we can describe the main kind of provisions commonly found in labor agreements.

Most contracts start out by stating which union and employer are entering into the agreement, for example, Local 15 of the International Union of Operating Engineers, AFL–CIO, and Skyscraper Management, Inc. Another necessary fact is the definition of the bargaining unit, which employees are covered by the contract and which employers are excluded from coverage. Contracts do this in several ways. One way is to list the job titles and the departments that are covered and to list those that are excluded. Another way is to say that everyone is covered except those specifically excluded and to list the exclusions. A third variation is to state that the contract covers every job in the bargaining unit as it was certified by the National Labor Relations Board.

The size and extent of the bargaining unit are important to both the union and the employer. The union likes as many employees as possible in the bargaining unit; the employer usually prefers to limit the size of the unit—and the union's strength.

An essential provision of every labor agreement is union security, which provides a union with stability and also income. These clauses range from the legal minimum to the legal maximum under the law. The minimum amount of security for a union is what the Labor–Management Act provides: exclusive representation. This means that once the union has been certified by the National Labor Relations Board as representing a majority of employees in the appropriate bargaining unit, that union is the exclusive representative of all the employees in the unit for purposes of collective bargaining.

The maximum amount of union security used to be a closed shop, where the employer must hire and employ only union members. The closed shop, however, is illegal under the Labor–Management Relations Act but it is permitted in the building construction industry. What happened was this: the Taft-Hartley Act of 1947 (The Labor–Management Relations Act) had banned *all* closed shops, but recognizing the special conditions in the construction industry, the Landrum-Griffin Act of 1959 amended the Labor–Management Relations Act to permit a form of closed shop in building construction.

The maximum amount of union security permitted under federal law is the union shop where employees must join the union in a specified time after being hired or after the union shop contract has been signed. The minimum amount of time, according to law, is thirty days. (In the building construction industry the period is seven days, thus providing, in effect, a closed shop.)

Even in a union shop, however, employees who have religious scruples about union membership need not actually join or be active in the union, but they must pay the equivalent of union dues and the initiation fee.

Another form of security is the agency shop. Non-union employees are not required to join the union but are required to pay dues or service charges to the union.

Additional union security is provided by contracts calling for the checkoff of union dues and fees. This is the system under which the employer deducts the sums from the pay of union members in the bargaining unit and turns them over to the union.

Under the federal law each employee must voluntarily give the employer an authorization in writing to deduct union dues and assessments and turn them over to the union. The authorization is valid for one year or the termination of the union contract, whichever occurs first. A checkoff provision may be used in conjunction with an agency shop or union shop contract.

A checkoff clause is very valuable to a union since it provides an assured income. The union is spared the effort and expense of chasing after members who are delinquent in their obligations and trying to collect back dues and assessments from them.

Related to the checkoff is another kind of union security: maintenance of membership. This provision dates back to World War II when employer and labor members of the National War Labor Board held conflicting views on the extent of union security. Labor favored the closed shop, management the open shop. As a compromise, they devised maintenance of membership which stated that employees who were union members or who joined the union had to maintain their membership for the duration of the contract. A fifteen-day escape period was provided in which employees could decide whether or not they wanted to stay in the union.

Under the right-to-work laws of some states, the union shop, the checkoff, and the maintenance of membership provision are illegal, even though they are permissable under the federal statute. The reason is an unusual provision in the Taft–Hartley Act which states:

"Nothing in this act shall be construed as authorizing the execution or application of agreements requiring membership in a labor organization as a condition of employment in any state or territory in which such execution or application is prohibited by state or territorial law." The states with these laws banning any form of compulsory union membership are generally in the South and Southwest, and are not, as yet, heavily industrialized. The existence of these laws may hamper union organizing efforts but it has not stopped them. Texas, one of the right-to-work states, is a current target for unionization.

One of the basic principles of unions is seniority—length of service—the belief that the longer a worker's service with a company, the greater his rights. These rights affect such employment conditions as the length of vacation, sick leave or personal leave, priority in choice of vacation period, promotions, transfers, and layoffs. Each worker exercises in seniority in relation to the seniority of other workers.

Contract provisions may cover the kind of seniority at the company and detail how seniority applies in specific situations. Among the kinds of seniority are: in the company, in a particular plant, in a department, or in an occupation. For example companywide seniority may govern the amount of vacation to which an employee is entitled, but his priority in choosing his vacation period may depend on his length of service in his department. Seniority in an occupation may apply to a layoff; for instance if a company must cut back the number of people in a specific occupation, it may do so on the basis of an individual's length of service in that job, not his length of service in the company. Whatever method the company follows will have been set forth in the contract. In a non-union company management can lay off whomever it chooses; senior employees have no special status or protection.

Automatic wage increases may be based partly or completely on seniority. Promotions, too, are very often dependent on seniority. Unions ordinarily prefer to have seniority as the only determining factor in promotion; companies prefer to base promotion on the individual's ability. Sometimes the contract contains a compromise: Promotions will be based on seniority if ability is equal. How ability is measured or whether the employer has measured ability fairly often leads to disputes between union and employer, disputes that may go to arbitration for resolution.

The term "super seniority" is also used. This usually refers to preferential seniority granted to union shop stewards who, regardless of their seniority, are protected against layoff so that so long as any union members are on the job they will have union representation familiar with them and the company. Seniority provisions may also cover situations where seniority may be broken or interrupted.

Another essential feature of a union contract is its protection against unfair or unwarranted discharge or discipline. In non-union organizations an employee can be fired for any reason or no reason, so long as the discharge is not for any reason that would be illegal, for example, any form of discrimination forbidden by law. Even then, if an employee suspects that the discharge (or any other unfair treatment) was for discriminatory reasons, the employee must file a complaint with the proper agency and await the outcome. In the meantime he or she is out of a job.

When a union contract exists the disciplined or discharged employee is almost certain to file a grievance. The precise ways in which the grievance procedures operate at various companies differ, but where a union contract exists, some form of grievance procedure exists. The grievance procedure assures the employee a review of his complaint up through the various steps of the procedure and the levels of union and management and to arbitration, if need be. The union is bound to take up the grievance; if it refuses, it may be found to be discriminating illegally. Or, under the Labor–Management Relations Act the employee can take up his grievance on his own with the employer and without the union representative and reach an adjustment "not inconsistent with the terms of a collective-bargaining contract . . ." The union representative must be given an opportunity to be present at the adjustment. Unless the union wants to be given an adjustment it does not like, it would, naturally, prefer to handle the grievance in its usual way.

Some non-union companies have a formal grievance procedure. An employee has to judge for himself whether the procedure can be helpful or whether it is simply an attempt to provide a semblance of "due process." However, the word of management is final. The right to arbitration by an outside impartial person simply does not exist.

Contracts also come to an end. Every contract states not only when it becomes effective but how long its duration will be. Procedures for renewal generally are included. Also, under the Labor–Management Relations Act, when either party to an existing contract wants to terminate or modify the contract, it must notify the other party in writing sixty days before the expiration date of the contract; or, if no expiration date exists, sixty days before it proposes to make the modification or terminate the contract. The Federal Mediation and Conciliation Service and any appropriate state agency must be notified thirty days after this, if no agreement has been reached. The agreement then continues, in effect, without strike or lockout for another sixty days after the notice is given or until the contract does end, whichever date is later.

The heart of a contract, as far as individual members are concerned, is the wage provision. For most of us, whether we are union members or not, the amount of money we receive for the time and effort expended on the job is important. In a sense, therefore, everyone who works for a living has a kind of contract with the employer: for so much per hour, day, week, month, year—or any other time—or for so many units produced, sold, or reviewed in a period of time, we will be paid an agreed-upon sum. The union contract does not change this. What it does do is formalize the terms.

Under a labor agreement the amount to be paid is specified, the conditions under which an increase may be given are specified. The wage may be a single rate, for example, $11.15 per hour to an electrician. Or the wages may be expressed as rate ranges. For instance the minimum rate per hour may be $3.95, while the maximum hourly rate for the same job may be $5.925. The actual job structure, the relations of each job to all others in the company, may be detailed in a plan based upon job evaluation. You may comment that the orderly arrangement of jobs in a classification scheme based on job evaluation can be found in many companies, institutions, or government agencies that are not unionized. True. But what a union does is bargain over the pay levels, negotiate the rates or the rate ranges. In a non-union organization the employer sets the rates unilaterally. When collective bargaining is involved, the union always talks about the pay levels. Even in a recession, when some companies seek concessions from their unions so as to stay in business, the union will be concerned about the wage or the salary level.

Because wage bargaining is central to unionization, union members regard wage negotiations as the main chance for getting a pay increase. This may explain why when you read or hear about contract talks that the union's wage demands may seem absolutely ridiculous. The union and employer know the first wage demands are not likely to be what they settle on; but the demands set boundaries. Whatever the union can wrest out of the employer is immediately visible to its members; if the wage increases look good, the union looks good, and the union officials look good—and they may stay in office.

Whatever wage gains are negotiated become part of the contract. An increase may cover all union members equally: so many cents per hour or dollars per week or a set percentage of the hourly rate. A percentage increase favors the higher-paid workers; a cents-per-hour increase favors the lower-paid workers.

An increase resulting from negotiations and given to all or most workers is called a general wage increase an across-the-board increase. Sometimes the union negotiates different increases for different job classes or groups, or an increase of so much now and so much at specified dates in the future. No matter what the union negotiates, the pay increases or changes become part of the contract. In companies where wages are based on incentive plans, that is upon units of production at or above a standard of output (piece rates, for instance), the union may bargain for changes in the rate or changes in the standard.

Often, when a company has both union and non-union employees, the increase given the union workers as a result of bargaining is passed along to the non-union employees as well. The increases in the unionized companies also affect non-unionized organizations. When pay levels in an industry or community rise because of collective bargaining, the non-unionized companies may find it difficult to keep or attract employees unless their pay levels are comparable. If they choose not to increase pay, they may give the unions ammunition to use against them in organizing drives.

Before leaving pay levels and increases a word about cost-of-living increases: these are increases based on changes in the Consumer Price Index issued by the Bureau of Labor Statistics in the U.S. Department of Labor. Many non-union companies take notice of these changes when setting pay rates, but some union contracts require corresponding changes in pay at specified times. If the contract runs for three years it may provide for an annual reopening to adjust wage rates according to changes in the Consumer Price Index.

So far, we have seen how wage provisions affect the entire union group, the bargaining unit. What about the individual employee? To the individual the wage provisions may be of most importance to the extent that they determine how he or she can get a raise in pay. A non-union company may give merit increases, which are determined largely by a superior's periodic review of your job performance, his or her determination of whether you deserve an increase, and, if so, how much. Some companies have no systematic method for granting increases and the employee must ask for and negotiate pay raises on his own, just as managerial and professional employees do.

For employees under a union contract the agreement sets forth the terms on which increases are granted. Unions generally favor automatic increases based on seniority. The contract may include a wage rate schedule showing a hiring rate or a minimum rate and detailing when an employee is entitled to an increase (after six months, after one year and so forth) and how much that increase will be (thirty-five cents per hour, fifteen dollars per week).

Another wage feature that may be found in a union contract states how much an employee will be paid if he or she performs a higher level job for a temporary period or if promoted or transferred.

In discussing wages, the various kinds of premium pay, call-in, and call-back pay, need noting. *Premium pay* is the term used to cover extra pay for working overtime, for working on a holiday or other day off, for hazardous work, or for working at an inconvenient time. The Fair Labor Standards Act (Wage and Hour Act) requires the payment of time-and-one-half the regular rate of pay for hours worked beyond forty in the workweek. The law covers most rank-and-file workers (certain kinds of employees and certain kinds of business fall under exemptions), but the law does not prevent a union from negotiating more than the law requires.

Instead of time-and-one-half for hours over forty, a union may negotiate premium pay for hours over seven or eight a day, or after thirty-five hours a week. Also common is a contract clause providing double time or more for work on a Saturday, Sunday, or holiday as such. (Some contracts specify the method for assigning or distributing overtime work.) *Call-in pay* covers situation where an employee reports to work as scheduled but is sent home because there is not enough work to do, and when a worker is called in on a day off to do some amount of work. In these cases contracts usually provide a minimum guarantee no matter how few the hours actually worked. *Call-back pay* is a guarantee of extra pay, generally at a premium rate, to employees who are called back to work after they have finished their regular assignments. Premium pay may be given for dangerous work or for especially unpleasant or dirty work. It frequently is given, in shift operations, to workers on the second or third shifts.

The wage provisions, and some variations on them, described above are found in most agreements in greater or lesser detail.

Vacations, holidays, and related benefits are very much part of the entire employment situation. In a unionized organization these provisions constitute an important part of the contract. Here is a list of the major reasons why pay may be given for unworked time:

> Vacations
> Holidays
> Personal leave
> Sick leave
> Jury duty or court attendance as a witness
> Death in the family
> Military training or reserve duty
> Tuition refund plans

Vacation pay and holiday pay are given all employees who meet whatever standards of eligibility the contract states. Usually, the length of vacation and the pick of vacation time are based on seniority. Vacation periods may be specified and such subjects as a holiday falling within the vacation period or an illness or accident occurring are dealt with. Holidays vary in number; like vacations, holiday pay may be governed by certain conditions, for example, the requirement that an employee work the scheduled day before or after the holiday. Personal leave or floating holidays are becoming more common. These give employees time off with pay to do with as they wish, without having to give reasons to a supervisor. Ordinarily these days off must be scheduled in advance and be approved by the supervisor so that work will not be disrupted.

The other kinds of paid time off are available to employees who require them. Paid sick leave is generally provided by a contract. As with vacation time, the amount of sick leave available to an employee usually depends on seniority. Limitations are set to prevent abuse of sick leave. The other provisions for paid time off vary from contract to contract and also are subject to restrictions. For instance some employers let employees keep whatever pay they get for jury duty; others pay the difference between the jury duty pay and the employee's regular wages; some give the time off (this is required by law) but do not give pay for it. The trend in union contracts has been to more time off with pay. However, some companies in a poor financial condition have been asking for "give-backs," and some unions have relinquished a portion of time off with pay.

As we know, paid time off is not the exclusive privilege of union members. Almost every company—regardless of size—institutions, and government agencies provide various forms of time off with pay. They may even outline the conditions under which time off is granted, and employees can rely on what the employer states.

The difference, when a union is present, is that the employer cannot change any conditions or any privilige without consulting the union. For instance when a unionized company in financial difficulties wants to cut down the number of personal-leave days, it must negotiate the change with the union. In a non-union company, if an employee believes his supervisor has interpreted a provision incorrectly, he generally can take his complaint up with his supervisor or with higher management. But whatever their decision, he must accept it or resign. In a unionized company an employee who thought he was not treated fairly, or consistently, would file a grievance. His union representative would then step into the situation and help him pursue his complaint through the formal grievance procedure, right up to arbitration by a neutral outside party, if necessary.

Other clauses in a labor agreement that have a dollar value or the employee are those providing an income in case of disability, or old age, or for payment of costs connected with keeping him and his family in good health. In this area of employee benefits the unionized companies in the private sector generally led the way. The trend grew, in particular, during and after World War II. During World War II wage and price controls were in effect. Wage increases were held down since they would contribute to the operating costs of war production and to inflation. Casting about for ways to give the unions some share in the profits industry was making, the War Labor Board came up with—along with unions and management—the idea of granting benefits that would not have an immediate impact on inflation, for instance, health insurance paid for by the employer. Since these were not part of the basic wage they were "fringes."

In the United States that, unlike Canada, has no national health insurance, the various components of health protection are very important bargaining issues. Some unions have a long history of concern over the health of their members. Others have in recent years, gone to great lengths to provide health and welfare benefits by actually setting up health facilities themselves. In New York the International Ladies' Garment Workers has elaborate and highly sophisticated facilities where union members come for regularly scheduled medical examinations and for treatment. Other unions have similar setups. The facilities are partly supported by contractual arrangements with employers in the industry, who pay a specified sum or percentage per employee to the union health and welfare plan. Another contractual arrangement requires the employer to supply a specified kind of insurance and welfare coverage for hospitalization, medical-surgical, dental, optical, major medical, long-term disability, life, retirement, etc. How generous or how restricted the plan, whether the employee contributes any part of the cost and, if so, how much,depends on collective bargaining. In other unions instead of the employer buying the various kinds of insurance required, the union selects and buys insurance coverage. Again, the employer supplies all or part of the cost through contributions based on the number of union members on his payroll.

The kinds of insurance, the extent of the coverage, whether spouses and family are covered, whether retired employees are covered, all depends upon negotiations with the employer. Naturally unions try to broaden coverage, to obtain more generous benefits. Employers usually try to hold the line. As you would expect, the trend is toward more; more kinds of protection, more liberal provisions.

Pension plans, it must be emphasized, also are significant parts of the welfare provisions provided by many contracts. Many variations exist, but all pension plans, as well as the health and welfare plans, are subject to the provisions of the Employee Retirement Income Security Act of 1974. This act does not mandate retirement plans; it simply sets the conditions under which new plans or existing plans must operate, provides for disclosure of plan details (including health and welfare plans), and guarantees some protection for employees with existing pension plans if the plan is discontinued.

As is the case with wages, benefits the unions obtain ordinarily are passed along to non-union employees either at the same company or in other firms. In the unionized sector, however, all these benefits are subject to collective bargaining. The employer cannot alter any plan, even to make it more generous, without negotiating with the union.

CHAPTER 11

What is Collective Bargaining?

Collective bargaining is the major function of a labor union. The union has other functions, too, which are described elsewhere in this book, but bargaining collectively is the reason for a union; it is essential to true unionism.

The dictionary definition is not really adequate: "Negotiation between an employer and union representatives on wages, hours, and working conditions." This sounds as if all collective bargaining involves is the one-time negotiation of an agreement. The opposite parties sit down for a few days or a number of weeks. After peaceful discussions or noisy arguments they emerge with a contract. That's it; collective bargaining is over for another year or so.

Collective bargaining goes on all during the contract period. It goes on every day, not merely once a year or once every two or three years. For once an agreement is in effect between employer and union, many issues arise that require additional discussion, additional bargaining. Collective bargaining is a continuing process.

No contract can cover all possible contingencies. Day-to-day happenings may call for further bargaining so that the intent of the basic agreement can be clarified or implemented or so that mutually acceptable interpretations can be made.

Collective bargaining also covers the resolution of grievances under the procedure specified in the contract. As we shall see one of the significant differences between unionized and non-unionized employment is that a union contract contains formal procedures for adjusting the grievances of employees (and of employers, too, in some instances).

Bargaining implies a give and take between two parties with the aim of reaching a settlement or a bargain that both can accept, even if each party must give up a portion of what it wishes to retain.

Even in a non-employment situation bargaining is not unknown to us. When you bring your five-year-old automobile to the local dealer hoping for a good trade-in allowance you probably will indulge in some bargaining with him. You may visit and bargain with several dealers before you strike the best bargain you can. You may not get as much as you wanted; the dealer may have given you more than his first offer, but you have struck your bargain. In some cultures bargaining is a way of life. In a Middle Eastern bazaar, for example, goods do not have a price tag attached. Buyer and seller expect to bargain before the trade is made.

Bargaining, therefore, is neither new nor novel, although collective bargaining in labor relations is. The word ''collective'' is the key. That union representative—or group of representatives—sitting down with the employer or his representatives takes the place of the entire group of employees, the members of the local union or the bargaining unit.

Once the employer has recognized the union voluntarily or once the National Labor Relations Board or a State Labor Relations Board has certified a specific union as the representative of a group of employees (or a bargaining unit) the union official at the bargaining table represents all those employees, whether there are sixty of them, six hundred or six thousand. That is collective bargaining.

Today bargaining is collective on the part of the employer. There are some company owners who speak for themselves, but most businesses now are corporations. Professional managers represent the company in negotiations; they speak in the name of the board of directors who speak in the name of the stockholders. In some cases a number of employers are represented by an association, which speaks for all members in negotiating with one or more unions.

Collective bargaining is public policy in the United States and Canada. This means that it is an activity encouraged by law, protected by law, and subject to law. The safeguarding by government of the right to bargain collectively is of comparatively recent origin, although unions have existed in the United States since the eighteenth century and in Canada since the nineteenth century.

Only since 1935 (in the United States) has unionism in the private industrial sector received any government encouragement and assistance. (Railroad unions in the United States came under the law in 1926.) Before that the history of the labor movement in the United States was a rough and often bloody one. Private and public attitudes ranged from hostile opinions to active opposition, frequently accompanied by violence and bloodshed. Whatever one's views may be, it is important to remember that in the United States and Canada unions now exist within the framework of law. Every union activity, from the first recognition by an employer throughout the whole relationship to the possible rejection or dissolution of a labor union, is subject to law.

In the United States the first expression of public policy toward collective bargaining in general was in Section 2 of the Norris-La Guardia Anti-Injunction Act of 1932.

Whereas under prevailing economic conditions, developed with the aid of governmental authority for owners of property to organize in the corporate and other form of ownership association, the individual unorganized worker is commonly helpless to exercise actual liberty of contract and to protect his freedom of labor, and thereby to obtain acceptable terms and conditions of employment, therefore, though he should be free to decline to associate with his fellows, it is necessary that he have full freedom of association, self-organization, and designation of representatives of his own choosing, to negotiate the terms and conditions of his employment, and that he shall be free from the interference, restraint, or coercion of employers of labor, or their agents, in the designation of such representatives or in self-organization or in other concerted activities for the purpose of collective bargaining or other mutual aid or protection. . . .

Note the phrase "designation of representatives of his own choosing to negotiate the terms and conditions of his employment." This introduces another point about unions which is often misunderstood: the principle of majority rule. If a union is designated by the majority of the people in an appropriate bargaining unit "to negotiate the terms and conditions of employment" it represents *all* the people in that unit. If a bargaining unit contains one hundred employees and fifty-one voted for the union while forty-nine voted for no union, the union represents all the people in that unit. The forty-nine who did not want the union cannot bargain for themselves or go shopping for another union they might like better. Although this is an oversimplification it illustrates the principle of majority rule, the principle, by the way, on which the governments of the United States and Canada are based. It is a principle that can create problems for both majority and minority. Any union that wants to stay in power must, like governments, be cognizant of the desires of the minority.

The techniques of collective bargaining are many and varied, depending on the economic conditions, the history, if any, of labor relations between employer and union and in the industry, the political climate, and the personalities on both sides of the bargaining table. Obviously, bargaining for a first contract will be different from the bargaining between a union and employer who have had a twenty-year relationship. And if that relationship was relatively amicable, the bargaining will differ from that between union and employer who have always been bitter adversaries. The recent bargaining in industries suffering from economic woes has been described as occurring in ''mature'' or ''sophisticated'' relationships.

What happens once the two sides start negotiations depends on the factors stated above. Some sessions are mere window dressing. Both employer and union representatives are experienced hands, know each other's strengths and weaknesses, and have a pretty good idea of where they will come out. But either or both sides may put on a show for the benefit of their audiences. Union officers are elected and are supposed to work hard for their members—and, by the way, for reelection. Even if the bargaining is not especially difficult, they must appear to have wrested contract improvements from the company at great difficulty so as to impress their membership. If the bargaining is over too quickly and looks too easy, the members may feel that they were shortchanged, that a more aggressive bargaining team would have won greater contract concessions. Management representatives often face the same situation. Vice presidents of industrial relations also have to earn their keep. One who has a good ongoing relationship with the union and who can bring negotiations to a satisfactory conclusion for the company is a valued executive, but if he appears to concede too easily or too quickly, his superiors may doubt his ability.

On the other hand many negotiations are genuinely difficult and complex; negotiations are arduous and agreement seemingly unattainable. One or both sides may be stubborn and inflexible; each party may be absolutely convinced that its position is the only right and rational one. Some of the issues to be resolved may be complicated; some may run counter to company or union policy. Any impasse—to be resolved only under threat of a strike or after a strike—may result. Occassionally, the unresolved issues may go to an imparital third party, an outsider, for settlement. Both unions and companies tend to resist third party resolution (usually by an arbitrator) because this third party is an outsider who does not have the intimate, firsthand knowledge of the employer and the union. Arbitration over contract negotiation, therefore, is rare.

The government also has a role under the labor law; (Labor–Management Relations Act of 1947 as amended, Sec. 8[d]) before a strike or lockout can occur in a dispute over the termination or modification of an existing contract, sixty days' notice must be given to the other party. Within thirty days after this notice the Federal Mediation and Conciliation Service and the appropriate state agency must be notified.

In effect this provides either a sixty-day cooling off period or sixty more days in which to attempt to reach agreement.

The Federal Mediation and Conciliation Service can offer its services to help mediate the dispute or the parties in conflict may request help. State mediation efforts can be sought on the same voluntary basis.

Mention should be made of another kind of bargaining agreement, one that is dishonest and contrary to law (although difficult to prove). This is a "sweetheart" contract. Here, union and employer connive to deprive employees of their rights. For a consideration the union officers will agree to a contract with substandard wages and benefits, or to a contract that will not be enforced, or to one negotiated by a "racketeer" union, or a union of whose existence the employees are unaware. Employees who are barely literate or who are foreign-born and do not understand English can be taken advantage of in this way. The union, in these cases, does not represent them and protect their legal rights, but the union officials do profit from the deal with the employer.

What the union usually brings to the bargaining table is a list of demands. Anyone who reads newspaper accounts of the current major bargaining activities knows that some of these demands sound outrageous, even ridiculous, at first reading. However, some demands that seemed extravagant or excessive a few years ago now are accepted terms of employment not only in unionized companies but in non-union ones as well. Our notions of excess or extravagance change with the times.

Where do demands come from? Unions must represent *all* members; the demands frequently do. The list drawn up by the union generally incorporates the wishes of its members. In some unions the list of demands must be ratified or approved before going to the employer. Many members have pet demands that they insist upon year in and year out, even though they realize they are impractical or impossible to realize. Or the union leaders who know that the employer cannot afford and will never agree to an improbable wage hike still must placate a membership that threatens to get out of control. And, again, ideas that seemed extreme in the past turn out to be logical, practical, and desirable; for example, consider provisions for dental- or optical-care benefits, very rare twenty-five years ago.

Some union officials paint themselves into a corner by going into bargaining with demands they know are completely unrealistic. Why? Because they may be trying to hold onto their positions of leadership by making extravagant promises to their members, promises which cannot be kept. A strike may result from such a situation. A frequently heard objection to union demands is that the union does not realize or is not concerned about whether an employer can meet demands and still stay in business at a profit. One answer is that unions recently have shown that they are concerned and do care, by moderating their demands and even giving up hard-won benefits.

Another answer is that operating a business at a profit is a managerial concern. The rank-and-file workers in the union do not set policies on what product to research, design, and produce; they are not responsible for choice of tools, techniques, materials, or methods; they do not formulate marketing plans. These are management responsibilities. If management makes serious mistakes and incurs heavy losses, it is the rank-and-file workers who are laid off first. They suffer the consequences of management's poor judgment or poor planning; why, then, should they worry greatly if management finds it difficult to agree to economic demands? Management also comes to the bargaining table with proposals or counter-proposals. The law requires both sides to bargain in good faith; they do not have to agree, but they do have to discuss and consider.

Recent events have shown that unions are not unaware of management's problems nor immune to logic. In an industry that has suffered great economic distress, the automobile industry, the concept of collective bargaining reached a new point, the union realizing that its health depended upon the recovery of the industry.

At the Chrysler Corporation, the President of the International Union of Automobile Workers, Douglas Fraser, was on the board of directors; the union thus shared some of the responsibility for managerial decisions. In bargaining with the other manufacturers, as well as with Chrysler, the International Union of Automobile Workers agreed to give up benefits it had gained in earlier negotiations to help the companies survive in a difficult competitive situation and in a recession and to afford union members, in particular the senior workers, stronger job security.

Union members did not give overwhelming support to the agreements at General Motors and at the Ford Motor Company, but the majority voted to ratify the agreements.

The New York Times of April 10, 1982, quoted the chief negotiator for General Motors, Alfred S. Warren, Jr.: "This contract opens a new chapter in American labor relations and clearly signals a move for us in a new direction—away from confrontation and toward cooperation, away from our adversarial past and toward a new alliance aimed at maintaining a competitive leadership in our products and assuring job security for all our employees."

A sidelight: General Motors was planning to give a bonus to executives. The union protested, pointing out that the rank-and-file had made sacrifices. The company saw the logic; no bonuses were given.

The law, which encourages collective bargaining, does more than simply state its wishes that union and company engage in ''good faith'' bargaining. A refusal to bargain, by either party, once the union is the legitimate representative of the employees, is an unfair labor practice and subjects the offending party to the remedial provisions of the law.

The actions or the words that constitute a refusal to bargain have been determined over the years through the orders of the National Labor Relations Board and through court decisions.

The initial objective of collective bargaining is the achievement of a contract between employer and union, setting forth the terms and conditions of employment for the employees represented by the union. If bargaining breaks down, mediation or arbitration can be restored to; if all peaceful attempts fail, a strike is possible.

CHAPTER 12

Strikes and Peaceful Settlement

Say the word "union" and many people respond with the thought "strike." Since strikes, picket lines of chanting workers and perhaps violent conduct, are undeniably more dramatic than day-in, day-out peaceful union activity, they make the headlines. Yet thousands of disputes between unions and employers are settled peaceably, without strikes or lockouts, by grievance procedures, mediation, and arbitration.

Some strikes are completely legal, a protected concerted activity under the Labor–Management Relations Act. Other strikes are illegal, a violation of both the law and the contract. Circumstances often determine the legality of a strike. For example if a contract has a no-strike clause, requiring that disputes be submitted, instead, to an arbitrator, the union that strikes rather than arbitrates is probably engaged in an illegal strike. If a group of employees decides to walk off the job as a protest without the sanction of the union and without regard for the contract their action is a wildcat strike and illegal. If the union approves of and calls a strike for an illegal purpose, the strike is illegal. For example let us say a union calls a strike to keep members of a racial minority group from working with them. Discrimination is forbidden by law; trying to force the employer to violate the law is an illegal strike.

The Labor–Management Relations Act (Section eight [b]) specifically forbids, as an unfair labor practice, certain strikes and boycotts where the object is illegal, such as forcing an employer or self-employed person to join a labor or employer association or enter into an illegal agreement, forcing someone to cease using products or doing business with anyone, forcing an employer to recognize or bargain with a union unless the union was certified by the National Labor Relations Board, forcing an employer to recognize and bargain with a particular union when another has been certified by the National Labor Relations Board, forcing an employer to comply with the union's demands in a union jurisdictional dispute.

In some cases the violations of the law seem clear but in most instances when an unfair labor practice such as an illegal strike is alleged, it takes a National Labor Relations Board investigation to determine whether a violation did occur.

Strikes are often legal, too. When a contract has ended and a new contract is being negotiated, bargaining efforts may break down. To exert pressure on the employer the union may call a strike. This is an economic strike and is the more common kind of strike.

When a union has been certified by the National Labor Relations Board as the representative of employees in the bargaining unit and the employer refuses to sit down and negotiate, the union may call a strike. This is an unfair labor practice strike.

The distinction between economic strikes and unfair labor practice strikes is important to the strikers. Economic strikers cannot be discharged, but they can be replaced. Unfair labor practice strikers can neither be discharged nor replaced. When workers strike they intend a temporary not a permanent work stoppage. And they intend to return to their jobs.

These are merely two examples of strikes that generally are

legal. Of course a strike may be legal, but the union or its members may still engage in unlawful activities, such as acts of violence against other workers or destruction of plant property.

Strikes are not undertaken lightly. The local union must have the backing of the members to run and man a strike. The usual procedure is to take a strike vote for approval by a majority, three fourths or two thirds of the members. The number depends on the local or international constitution. If a majority of the union members approve, the local's leaders have a stronger position at the bargaining table. That a strike vote is taken does not mean that a strike will be called, but it does serve to show management that the union is prepared to use its most potent weapon. The local, however, must also look to its international union. Almost all unions require a local to have the approval of its international before striking. The reasons are practical ones. The international union sets the standards; it knows what bargaining goals it intends to achieve; if a local union gets out of line it can damage the international. Also, the need for approval by the international can keep a local union from acting irresponsibly, perhaps by calling for an illegal work stoppage, pulling a strike when it has no chance of winning, or striking at a time when economic or other conditions are not favorable. The approval of the international also means that financial support may be forthcoming from the international's strike funds. Sometimes a local strikes first and gets approval from its international later.

Finances are extremely important to a union considering a strike. Union members may have to do without regular income for a period of time. The union really needs a full war chest when it considers strike action. Actually, unions plan very carefully when a strike is contemplated. The timing is important. If the company has low inventories and a high backlog of orders, a strike can be persuasive. The point is that a strike whether by a craft union or an industrial union is not a lark; it is serious and must be properly planned. That the members show support by endorsing a strike does not mean that their enthusiasm or morale will survive a long strike. Sometimes they approve a strike without realizing the price they must pay or that the strike may result in the union's making concessions. A strike places a burden on the union leadership. If the stoppage is successful and they come back with concessions from the employer, so much the better. But if the leaders must give ground and since they are closer to the realities of the situation they may be forced to, they must face a disappointed membership and even loss of office. These days, too, unions reflect a pluralistic society; members are not necessarily unanimous in their sentiments. A vocal minority may pull others along with its strike talk and militant attitude; if the strike continues for a longer time than anticipated, the less-than-enthusiastic members may be part of a back-to-work movement. There are times, however, when pressures build up within a union so that a strike almost is a necessary safety valve permitting workers to let off steam.

What are some of the items for which the union must plan? First of all, money. Members on strike must still eat and pay their bills. In most states they are not eligible for unemployment insurance benefits. The union needs funds for its members during a strike to help cover their basic needs. The workers themselves, of course, give up their paychecks, do picket line duty, perform other services, and try to cover living expenses out of their own savings. Most international unions and local unions build up strike funds. The money comes out of dues and assessments and is intended to cover not only nominal sums for the strikers and their families but any legal or other expenses that may arise. The union may also help its needy members to get welfare or food stamps. Frequently, other unions made contributions, particularly if the strike is one that engages their sympathies.

Another item the union considers is very important: picketing. If the first step in a work stoppage is to get union members off the job, a second step is to keep them off and keep anyone else from going in. A strike aims at a complete shutdown of activities. Picketing takes many forms, some legal and some illegal.

A picket is an individual, usually a union member, who stands or walks near or at the entrances and exits to a plant or a company. In a labor dispute, such as a strike, pickets generally form a line and march up, down, or around, as the case may be. All or many may carry placards notifying the public that a dispute exists. Their aim in a strike goes beyond providing information about a dispute; their intention is to persuade others not to go into the premises being picketed. The "others" may be timid union members afraid of losing their jobs, non-union workers, employees hired to replace strikers (strikebreakers or scabs), or truck drivers and others making deliveries to the plant or company.

The attitude of the law toward picketing has undergone changes since the days when all picketing was banned. Now, peaceful picketing at the scene of the primary industrial dispute generally is permitted. However, mass picketing that really is a blockade of the company by a solid group or mass of pickets does occur and it may be accompanied by physical violence. Although it is illegal under the Labor–Management Relations Act, mass picketing is an effective means of "persuasion." And to end it the employer must go to court. By the time he gets an injunction against it the mass picketing may have been successful.

Organizing a disciplined and effective picket line is, therefore, a major strike activity. Union members usually are given picket line assignments. Shop stewards act as picket line captains. Their picket line duties keep the strikers busy and help keep their morale up since they participate along with their fellow union members and gain the feeling of participation in a common cause for the common good. At strike headquarters, where pickets drop in on their way to and from the picket line, they have a chance to talk with each other, have a cup of coffee together, pick up the latest news, and have their spirits buoyed by union leaders.

Picketing is a form of publicity, but unions also seek other means of promoting good public relations. Some take out advertisements in local papers to proclaim the justice of their cause and the reasonableness of their demands. A spot on a local radio interview program or a television news program can be helpful. During the strike the union prepares special bulletins or fliers to keep members informed and spirits up. Mass meetings may be held, especially if support from other unions can be announced or some progress in negotiations seen.

Support from other unions is sought and valued; the assistance may be in the form of cash contributions or simply moral support. The union that gets no kind of assistance from others in the labor movement or that disregards the advice of more seasoned union leaders may find itself in difficulties. The 1981 strike of the Air Traffic Controllers in the United States was one such stoppage. Apparently the union not only misjudged the determination of the government to withstand the stoppage but also did not enlist the support of the labor movement. Added to these factors was the lack of any element of surprise or of catching the employer at a bad time; previous strike threats by the same union had given the government time to plan for the actual strike.

If a strike goes on for some time, it becomes increasingly important for the union to keep members from getting depressed or discouraged. Some unions organize recreation, set up a central cafeteria or even a soup kitchen, try to get wives and families involved in some of the activities, for example, helping with members who need assistance in emergencies.

A serious problem may be a back-to-work movement, often initiated through the employer's efforts. While the union has been busy planning and running a strike, the employer usually has not been idle. Just as the union gauges the best time for calling a work stoppage, the employer tries to anticipate his problems and see if he can afford to take a strike and if so for how long.

Even if a company is not producing, selling, and delivering a product, or providing a service, it still has overhead costs that a strike does not end. If a strike lasts for some time, it is possible that skilled employees will find other jobs and not want to return. Although supervisory employees may be able to replace the strikers, there comes a time when they cannot do more than keep up appearances. Repairs or maintenance of machinery or equipment may cease. Services to the public may suffer as backlogs of work pile up.

The back-to-work movement initiated by the company may effectively end a strike that has dragged on for a long time if the workers are suffering from loss of income or if their enthusiasm has waned. The workers may feel that some income is better than none and that returning to work is the sensible solution. If a back-to-work movement gains momentum, the union may lose the strike.

Like the union, the company may take the public relations route—advertisements and radio and television appearances. If you keep an eye out for the public relations aspects of a strike, you may derive some amusement from the fact that both sides, labor and management, always have the interests of the public at heart. The union never says its demands are excessive; management never says it is making an adequate profit. Both union and management are engaged in industrial strife, they feel, for the public good. This is not to denigrate the gravity of industrial disputes but rather to show the awareness both sides have of public opinion.

Both employer and union do have as their aim the resumption of business. A dispute keeps them apart; but both look to a resolution of it and a return to operations. In some plants, for example, the union picket line parts to let in the personnel who keep the equipment and machinery in working order, because the pickets anticipate going back to work and, when they do so, want no delays due to improper maintenance.

A strike usually ends when one side believes that holding out will hurt it more than giving in. (Some work stoppages, particularly those that involve an entire industry or may imperil national health and safety are subject to special provisions of the Labor–Management Relations Act.)

A strike may leave an aftermath of some bitterness; not all strikes are conducted peacefully; there may have been a considerable amount of emotion and hostility during the stoppage. But more often, both sides are eager to get down to normal business operatons. The union generally goes back to its members proclaiming the "victories" it has won. If any concessions were made, they generally are played down. The emphasis is on the great job the union leadership did for the members. Since in many cases the strike settlement or the new agreement must be approved by the members, the union leaders must be good salespeople, to persuade the rank-and-file to approve the settlement. These days, rank-and-file members may not go along with the leaders and may reject the agreement. Then it is back to the bargaining table again.

Nevertheless, current strike negotiations are ordinarily far different from those in the early days of the labor movement, even different from those forty or fifty years ago. In the past violence and bloodshed marked many labor disputes. Companies imported strikebreakers who created violence and provoked the union members to violence. Government officials often were persuaded to send in the troops to quell the violence. Usually, the presence of troops merely inflamed union sentiments and resulted in death and injury on both sides. The result was a wider gulf between industry and labor and a perpetuation of the adversary relationship. Over the years, as both industry and labor have become more accustomed to collective bargaining, a more cooperative and constructive attitude prevails, especially in big industry. Instead, for example, the current relationship is a cooperative one, yet some of the bloodiest battles between labor and management had occurred in that industry. Strikes are, of course, one means of using force to settle a disputed issue and they are the means most often resorted to. On its side management has the lockout. Employers, in a strike, try to shut down the plant. Other methods for settling disputes, available to either party, include injunctions to prevent breach of contract, lawsuits for damages, the voiding of a contract which has been violated, and in the case of alleged unfair labor practices by either employer or union, settlement by the National Labor Relations Board.

One important reason for the abatement of bitter strife and the more equable climate in labor relations is the presence of the grievance procedure, culminating in arbitration and in unionized industry. Even government bodies, where unions are forbidden to strike, have found the grievance procedure and arbitration a positive factor in labor relations.

Basically the grievance procedure provides employees and their union with an opportunity to present a grievance at various levels of the management hierarchy, to be heard. If the issue is not resolved, it can go to an outside, neutral third party, an arbitrator, for a final decision.

The number of steps in a grievance procedure, the number and levels of management and union people involved vary. As you would expect, the size and complexity of company and union influence the grievance procedure. In general an employee with a complaint first takes it up with his shop steward, who then sees the foreman or supervisor. At this stage the grievance may not be in writing, and the talk between union representative and company supervisor may be informal. If both are used to dealing with each other, they know their situation well enough to be candid with each other. Most grievances are settled at this stage.

Next, if the complaint has not been resolved, it usually gets put into writing and is then taken up by the union grievance committee and the next level of management, probably the personnel or industrial relations department. The union grievance committee consists of the local union president and other designated officials. In a craft union local the business agent is a committee member.

The next step, if the grievance is still not settled, is a meeting between top union officials, perhaps accompanied by a representative of the international union, and top management of the company.

We have thus far merely sketched in the framework of a three-step grievance procedure. As we mentioned, however, the procedure can vary; there may be five steps, for example. What does not vary is the route upward, from the lowest levels of union and management to the higher levels.

Often, the grievance procedure has a time table. Grievances must be submitted within a specified period of time. Management must answer within a specified period of time. If it does not, the grievance goes to the union by default. Under some grievance provisions, serious complaints, for example, those concerning a group of employees, bypass the first stages of the procedure and go directly to the higher steps.

The grievance procedure not only provides the individual employee with a chance to get a fair hearing but also provides a means of contract interpretation. No written instrument can possibly foresee every possible situation that may arise in the future. When circumstances not expressly covered by the contract do occur, interpretation is necessary. Union and management may disagree as to the proper interpretation; through the grievance procedure their differences can be resolved.

The agreement, however, stands unless top management and top union officials agree to a change. The participants in the lower levels of the procedure cannot change policy; they can change a practice if they find it is in violation of the contract or is an incorrect interpretation or application of the agreement. (They can recommend changes; indeed, they often do suggest changes to be sought in the next negotiations.) Even an arbitrator cannot alter the contract. The only ones who can do so are the parties themselves, employer and union, through collective bargaining.

So important is the grievance procedure that the shop stewards, whose main job is investigation and handling of grievances, get time off with pay, during the work day, for those tasks. (They usually receive training from their unions in how to investigate and process grievances.)

The last step, no matter how many a particular grievance procedure includes, is voluntary arbitration. Almost every labor agreement—about ninety-five percent—contains a provision requiring arbitration of unresolved disputes or grievances. Usually, the clause providing for arbitration also provides that the union will not engage in a strike and the employer will not engage in a lockout. Thus, arbitration provides a peaceful means for dispute settlement.

In arbitration a third party, a neutral outsider chosen by the parties, determines the dispute. His determination is final and binding upon both parties. Whether the arbitration is conducted by a single arbitrator or a tripartite board, whether the arbitrator is selected for each arbitration as necessary (ad hoc arbitration), or whether the arbitrator or board of arbitrators is permanent, the principles are the same. Arbitration is a profession. Arbitrators are expected to be objective, knowledgeable about labor relations and labor law, and not identified with either management or unions. They are usually lawyers or college professors.

Arbitrators may act as mediators or conciliators, but mediation and conciliation are not the same as arbitration. The distinction is that a conciliator or a mediator does not hear evidence and render a decision. A conciliator is like a go-between, trying to bring the parties together, but not taking part in the process himself. A mediator takes a more active role, although he does not make a decision. He makes suggestions or recommendations, but it is up to the parties themselves to resolve their dispute.

The terms mediation and conciliation are used interchangeably as in the Federal Mediation and Conciliation Service. Conciliators and mediators usually are not chosen by the disputants, as an arbitrator is; they may be appointed by a state or federal agency or volunteer their services under federal or state law.

How do the parties find an arbitrator? Through the American Arbitration Association, the Federal Mediation and Conciliation Service, or state mediation agencies. These groups maintain panels or list of persons qualified by their standards to serve as arbitrators.

They supply the names and give qualifications to the parties who must agree on the choice of arbitrator. If after several lists are submitted the parties cannot agree on an arbitrator, the agency will choose one for them. When a tripartite board is required, each party selects one arbitrator and the two arbitrators choose the third impartial member.

A contract clause usually states when arbitration is to be invoked, the issues that may be submitted to arbitration, any limits upon the power of the arbitrator, and even the rules under which the arbitrator is to proceed. Most contract clauses permit any dispute or grievance to go to arbitration; others limit arbitration to disputes arising out of interpretation or application of the contract. In the prevailing industrial climate there is almost no subject that is not arbitrable under the phrase "interpretation and application of the agreement." Of course the parties may specify a subject that is not arbitrable. Some clauses restrict the power of the arbitrator, stating what he may not rule on. For instance, in a discipline case, the arbitrator may be limited to deciding whether the discipline was for "just cause" but not be able to reduce the penalty if he finds that "just cause" did exist.

Arbitrators are not to change the terms of a contract or to add or subtract from it. But their decisions certainly influence the interpretation and application of the contract. Arbitrators usually look to the contract first of all as the basis for a decision. If the contract is silent, the arbitrator may inquire into the past practice or custom in the company or industry to their negotiation history and, finally to current practice or industrial relations.

Arbitrators' decisions, which are called "awards," are generally in written form. The award states what the dispute was, how the arbitrator ruled, the reasons for his decision, what action must be taken to carry out the award, for example, reinstatement of the employee with back pay.

An arbitration award is final and binding upon both parties and can be enforced in court. An award cannot be overturned unless there is evidence of fraud or misconduct on the part of the arbitrator.

Strictly speaking, the arbitrator does not have to go into detail. He can write a one-paragraph decision. But an informative written award can be helpful to the employer and the union; it helps the union explain to its members, helps the company explain to its supervisors and managers, and may give both parties guidance useful in future negotiations. Having explained the virtues of a lengthy award, it is necessary to point out that in companies and industries with thousands of employees, a heavy volume of grievances, and a group of permanent arbiters who go from plant to plant hearing disputes, written awards of any length would be impossible.

An arbitrator's awards also are read with interest by the parties trying to choose an arbitrator. They keep a kind of box score: How many did the arbitrator decide in favor of the company? How many for the union? Unions and companies exchange information with each other about different arbitrators.

The importance of an award extends beyond an individual case. Awards now form a substantial body of labor relations information and are frequently termed "the common law" of labor relations. Discharge and discipline are the matters most often submitted to arbitration. Other issues often submitted include layoffs, seniority, and ability in promotion cases, paid holidays, vacations and vacation pay, overtime distribution, and discriminatory treatment.

Disputes over issues such as these listed above arise under an existing contract. Arbitration over the terms of a contract negotiation is rarer, but it does occur, and it is a peaceful alternative to a strike. The objection to such arbitration is that it gives to a third party the right to make decisions on terms and conditions of employment that the parties must live with but which they did not determine.

Arbitration is called a quasi-judicial process. Several states do have arbitration statutes. The arbitrator can subpoena witness and evidence; the hearing is conducted like an informal court hearing: witnesses are sworn in; exhibits marked; evidence presented. The arbitrator has wide latitude in deciding what evidence to consider.

Despite the absence of a federal statute decisions of the U.S. Supreme Court leave no doubt that a contractual agreement to arbitrate will be respected by the courts.

CHAPTER 13

Neighbor to the North

Some Americans think the only difference between the United States and Canada is geography. They are wrong. Although Canada, like the United States, has British roots, English is the native tongue, and Americans and Canadians pass freely from one country to the other without experiencing culture shock, significant differences between the two countries are reflected in their labor movements.

One difference is the French roots of a large part of Canada. A substantial portion of the population (over twenty-five percent) speaks a separate language, practices a different religion, is steeped in a different culture, and even lives to a large extent in one province, Quebec. A large part of the Canadian population is descended from people who settled in Canada before the English. (Canada had been claimed for France in the sixteenth century by Jacques Cartier. It did not become an English colony until the eighteenth century, before the American Revolution.) Before industrialization, the French Canadians were mainly a rural people. With the advent of industrialization, they provided the labor. The managerials, professional, and technical staffs were largely English-speaking. In Quebec, the English-speaking people were the minority. Thus the basis was established for class conflict and division that has exacerbated the labor movement as well as in other aspects of political, economic, and social life in Canada.

Canada had a longer period of dependence upon Great Britain— first as a colony, then as a dominion—than did the United States. The Canadian constitution went into effect in 1982, making Canada a separate country rather than a dominion in the British family of nations. Unlike the United States, Canada has no traditions deriving from a revolution for independence from Great Britain.

The Canadian economy also differs from that of the United States. It is less diversified than the American economy. A country of vast natural resources, Canada exports these in raw or semi-finished states. It is, therefore, an economy very much dependent on foreign trade and capital. The economy is more precarious, more subject to seasonal and cyclical variations. This in turn leads to unemployment and instability. Until recently, industrialization was limited, developing much later than in America. A large part of Canada's manufacturing industries did not develop until the twentieth century. Manufacturing did not go through the small-to-large stages familiar in the United States. Industries in Canada were large right from their beginnings, applying the mass production and technical expertise that had already been developed in Great Britain and the United States. With a small population and its limited purchasing power, Canada had room for only one or two firms in an industry. Major industries tended to be monopolistic.

In terms of the labor movement, union organization was difficult. Companies were scattered geographically. Their combination into large firms made them more resistant to union pressures. Until recently, according to Stuart Jamieson (*Industrial Relations in Canada*), Canadian employers were less willing than their American counterparts to recognize and make concessions to unions, although they expressed their opposition with less violence.

The Canadian government, both federal and provincial, in early legislation and in the legislation now in effect, places great emphasis on prevention of strikes and lockouts. Until fairly recently incidents of violence, illegality, or intervention by police or armed forces occured infrequently. Laws encouraging or protecting union activity, however, were not enacted until post-World War II. Moreover, Canada's federal system is extremely decentralized. The central government has less power than the American federal government and the provinces have much more power than the states. This prevents effective federal regulation over large private interests and effective economic planning at the national level. Federal jurisdiction in Canada covers industries employing less than ten percent of the labor force; ninety percent of the labor force is divided among ten provinces, each with their own statutes. Naturally, this increases the difficulties of union organization. Despite the early intervention of either federal or provincial governments in labor disputes, the level of industrial conflict, violence, and illegality, though lower than in America, is higher than in comparable countries.

Although trade unionism in Canada has a shorter history than in America, it is a complex history.* The early influence on Canadian labor came from Great Britain. Later, with improvements in communication and transportation, American influences were felt. The demands of the Civil War in the United States brought an economic boom to Canada. It was then that British influence began to ebb and American influence to increase. America was nearer; American unions began activities in Canada. Periodically, antagonism toward American influence flared up and sporadic attempts were made to organize federations of purely Canadian unions.

* Sources for this summary were: *Industrial Relations in Canada, 2nd ed.* by Stuart Jamieson, Toronto (Macmillan of Canada, 1973); *Labour Policy and Labour Economics in Canada,* by H. D. Woods and Sylvia Ostry, Toronto (Macmillan of Canada, 1962).

As early as the 1820s small local organizations called "labor circles" existed. The boot and shoe workers in Montreal organized in 1827. That same year, the printers in Quebec organized a combined trade union and mutual aid society. Other crafts began to organize: carpenters, coopers, and stone masons, for example. But until the middle of the century, these groups were few and purely local.

Trade unions developed rapidly from the 1850s to the 1870s, encouraged by similar progress in Great Britain and America. In Canada, much of the leadership and direction came from Great Britain by men who already had union experience. Shipwrights, sailmakers, caulkers, and moulders organized. British immigrants started branches of the Amalgamated Society of Carpenters and Joiners and the Society of Engineers (machinists).

The National Union of Iron Moulders, founded in Philadelphia in 1859, had locals in Toronto, Quebec City, Hamilton, London, and Brantford. A local printers' organization in St. John, New Brunswick, affiliated in 1865 with the International Typographical Union in the States. Development of rail transportation in Canada led to unionization. Brotherhoods of Engineers and Conductors of Firemen, and of Trainmen were organized from the 1860s to the 1880s, and were affiliated with the American international unions. Fifteen unions formed the Toronto Trades Assembly in 1871. The next year, the Toronto printers struck for a nine-hour day. Soon afterward, a number of union leaders were jailed for conspiracy. Widespread agitation arose among unionists and their supporters. The Canadian government passed new legislation, modelled on that of Great Britain, which freed unions from liability under the common law for conspiracy in restraint of trade.

A Canadian Labor Union, mainly confined to Ontario, was formed, but it could not survive the depression of the 1870s and was out of existence by the latter part of that decade. The Knights of Labor, however, grew rapidly in Canada and outlasted the American group by ten years. At the end of the 1880s, the Knights had about sixteen thousand Canadian members, two hundred fifty locals, and seven district assemblies. The Knights were especially well suited to Canadian operations, where trades and industries were semi-rural and scattered geographically. In Quebec, the Knights had at first been outlawed because their secret ritual was offensive to Catholics. But after the secrecy was abandoned and Cardinal Gibbons of Philadelphia persuaded the Pope to remove the ban, the Knights made rapid progress in Quebec.

In the meantime, the Toronto Trades Assembly had become the Toronto Trades and Labor Council and was trying to set up a federation. It met with the Knights of Labor and established the Canadian Labor Congress which had a very short life. In 1886, however, a new federation, the Dominion Trades and Labor Congress, was founded.

In 1892, the Dominion Trades and Labor Congress became the TLC (Trades and Labor Congress of Canada). At this time too, the 1880s, the American Federation of Labor had been organized. A bewildering series of splits and realignments took place after both AFL and TLC were in existence. Some unions shed their AFL affiliation either because of a real or imagined antipathy to American unionism or because of different regional or cultural interests.

In 1902, TLC changed its constitution so as to exclude unions that conflicted with AFL jurisdiction and to refuse representation to any city central organization that did not have a TLC charter. This resulted in expulsion of the Knights of Labor groups and also excluded some purely Canadian unions.

The TLC also met opposition in western Canada from Wobblies, the International Workers of the World. They had organized loggers, miners, and railroad workers in British Columbia and in Alberta. They lost ground after a number of bitter strikes, but they laid the foundation for a radical orientation of labor in western Canada that had repercussions in the nineteen twenties and thirties.

In 1921, after the wartime boom years, the economy in Canada collapsed. As in the United States, union membership declined.

That year, TLC expelled the Canadian Brotherhood of Railroad Employees (CBRE), the largest single trade union in Canada, on the grounds that it conflicted with the jurisdiction of the AFL Brotherhood of Railroad and Steamship Clerks. The expelled union, whose membership consisted of railroad employees outside of the operating crafts, took the lead in organizing a new labor congress.

The Western Labor Congress met in Calgary in 1919. Out of it came One Big Union (OBU), similar to the Wobblies. A general strike broke out in Winnipeg which had widespread support. By the end of 1919, OBU had almost forty-two thousand workers. TLC opposed it, as did federal and provincial authorities, and OBU gradually declined.

When the Knights of Labor were excluded from the TLC by its constitution, they joined with other Canadian unions to form the Canadian Federation of Labor in 1908. The Canadian Federation of Labor kept going until the early 1920s; its membership peaked in 1923 then declined. After World War I, CFL lost most of its locals in Quebec to TLC and to *syndicats catholiques;* the *syndicats* then formed a third competing labor congress of French-speaking Catholic workers.

In 1927, remnants of the OBU, the CFL, the CBRE, and a few other unions organized the All-Canadian Congress of Labor (ACCL). A nationalistic organization, it carried on vituperative campaigns against the TLC and affiliates of the American international unions, calling them ''alien,'' ''foreign,'' and ''Yankee-dominated.'' Communists formed the Workers' Unity League, which made some progress in British Columbia among the mining, smelting, textile, and auto workers. By 1934, this group had disbanded.

The passage of the National Labor Relations Act (Wagner Act) in the United States in 1935 reverberated in Canada. The Canadian Labor movement agitated for similar legislation. The rise of the Congress of Industrial Organizations had a similar effect. The TLC, with its ties to the AFL, had to expel CIO unions. It lost about twenty-thousand members and did not recover from loss of peak membership untilWorld War II. The ACCL also underwent strains during this time. Some of its affiliates withdrew and formed a new Canadian Federation of Labor which dwindled out. The OBU remnants left the ACCL, which resulted in the ACCL becoming a relatively small organization, with the CBRE as its only important union. A new, larger, and more stable federation grew out of the appeal of industrial unionism typified by the CIO. Seven Canadian branches of CIO unions joined the ACCL in 1940. The ACCL changed its constitution and its name, becoming the Canadian Congress of Labor (CCL).

The problem of communist domination of unions arose in Canada after World War II. In the CCL, bitter conflicts took place between executives and the pro-red opposition. Communists held positions of leadership in the International Woodworkers, the Mine, Mill and Smelter Workers, the Auto Workers, the Electrical Union, as well as in purely Canadian unions. Yet the anti-communist leadership prevailed.

In the more conservative TLC, after World War II, communists had responsible positions in several unions: Textile Workers, Chemical Workers, some building trades locals, the Canadian Seamen's Union, and the United Fishermen and Allied Workers.

From 1947 on, when the communist party line switched to opposition to established union leadership, both the CCL and the TLC experienced conflict. Spy trials, notably the Gouzenko case in Canada, turned opinion and communist influence waned. In 1949, the CCL expelled the Mine, Mill and Smelter Workers and it suspended officers of the United Electrical Workers from membership in the CCL executive council.

TLC had even more strains, particularly in its relationship with the AFL. In 1947 the AFL demanded that TLC convert the Canadian Seaman's Union into the Seafarer's International Union. TLC held out for two years before giving in. In 1949 the AFL again pressed TLC to eliminate every trace of communist control and influence. Eventually, TLC ended the affiliation of the Canadian Seaman's Union, but it did not admit the Seafarer's.

Union growth came to a halt in the early '50s. The merger of the AFL and CIO in America led to the 1956 merger of the TLC and the CCL into one organization, the Canadian Labor Congress (CLC). Then, as in the States, new, younger men came into positions of leadership. The rapidly growing number of public employees sought affiliation with organized labor. But a major problem remained: the separate French-speaking Catholic labor organization in Quebec. In that province, the *Confederation des Travailleurs Catholiques du Canada* (CTCC) had developed separately from other labor movements and had often been in conflict with them. This separate labor movement had its origins in the various church-sponsored Catholic labor federation in France, Belgium, and Holland before the first World War. Again, the cultural separation of Quebec from the other Canadian provinces must be remembered. In Quebec, eighty percent of the population was French-speaking; only twenty percent was English-speaking. Under the British North America Act, the province enjoyed a high degree of autonomy, with separate legal and educational systems.

The economy was agricultural. People lived not only in geographical but also social isolation. Rapid industrialization and urbanization threatened this distinct and rural way of life. Capital, technical expertise, and organization structure came from America and Great Britain, so the executive and technical positions in the corporate hierarchy tended to be filled by the English-speaking majority. But the French Canadians soon began to acquire the know-how. The 1960s saw the so-called "Quiet Revolution," with its tendency in Quebec toward modernization and secularization.

The CTCC had begun as a movement consciously organized and controlled by the church, which wished to keep the French Canadians from losing their own culture and language by being absorbed into unions controlled by the English-speaking Canadians and Americans. The Catholic unions in their early stages stressed cooperation and harmony with employers. Other unions accused the *syndicats* of undercutting their efforts, strikebreaking, and selling out to employers. In 1921 the *syndicats* officially adopted the name of *Confederation des Travailleurs Catholiques du Canada* (CTCC) and grew in membership during the nineteen thirties and World War II. The conflict between the two other Canadian federations, the TLC and the CCL, enabled the CTCC to survive although it was comparatively small.

Major changes took place after World War II. Industry expanded and the CTCC workers came into contact with others of differenct religions and ethnic roots as the CTCC unions got jurisdiction over new plants. The inequalities between what the CTCC unions gained and what the other unions had won became apparent. The Catholic unions became more militant under new and aggressive lay leaders, many of them graduates of Laval University.

As a result of the 1949 asbestos strike, which lasted seven months, the CTCC emerged with greater prestige and power than it formerly had. The Catholic Church hierarchy openly supported the strikers in their clash with the subsidiary of an American company after the provincial government had declared the strike illegal, decertified the union, and sent armed provincial police into the conflict. Widespread support came from the prominent liberal and intellectual leaders as well as from the TLC and CCL. In the nineteen fifties, the CTCC became the center of movements for political and social reform in Quebec. The CTCC also discussed the possibility of merger with the CLC, but nothing came of the talks. However, cooperation with each other was not ruled out. In 1957 the United Steel workers, for example, supported a strike of the copper mining and smelting workers in Quebec. The CTCC also picked up a number of CLC locals comprised of French-speaking radio and television employees after the Montreal strike against the Canadian Broadcasting Corporation in 1959. The French-speaking personnel felt that the CLC—and the federal government—were indifferent to the needs of the French-speaking staff members.

In 1960, the CTCC dropped all vestiges of connection with the Catholic Church and remained itself the *Confederatio des Syndicats Nationaux* (CSN) or in English, the Confederation of National Trade Unions (CNTU). The CSN grew rapidly in the '60s when new and more liberal labor codes were enacted. It made rapid gains among professional and salaried employees in public service. The view of its leaders also became more radical and separatist.

As the union movement in Canada grew, the laws concerning labor relations underwent changes also. Two major points must be stressed:

1. In Canada, the provinces posess more power than the central or federal government. This differs significantly from the situation in America.

2. In Canada, even in early legislation, emphasis is placed more upon intervention in disputes and restriction upon freedom to engage in strikes or lockouts. This also differs from America, where legislation first encouraged and protected collective bargaining and where government intervention is confined to national emergency strikes, under the Taft-Hartley Act.

Before World War II government policy was modeled on that of Great Britain as modified by Canadian experience. In provincial and federal legislation dating back to the 1870s a marked preoccupation existed, the attempt to settle disputes, prevent strikes, and avoid "public disorder" were foremost—protecting the rights, liberties, and prerogatives of the parties. Jamieson (*Industrial Relations in Canada*) believes this reflects an exaggerated view of the damage strikes could inflict on a vulnerable economy.

In discussing government attitudes toward labor unions in the

United States, the use of the common law doctrine of criminal conspiracy to defeat unionization was mentioned. Since American common law is derived from English common law, it is not surprising the doctrine then was utilized in Canada, too. However, in 1872 the Trades Union Act and the Criminal Law Amendment Act defined unions as legitimate voluntary associations and exempted them from charges of criminal conspiracy.

As early as the 1870s, Canadian provinces began to enact legislations for dispute settlement. Ontario, for instance, passed legislation in 1873 calling for boards of conciliation. (The Quebec Trades Dispute Act of 1901 remained in effect until 1964.)

In 1900, the federal government passed a Conciliation Act. Under it the Minister of Labor could appoint conciliation boards upon request of representatives of employer or employee. The first element of compulsory conciliation came with Railway Labor Disputes Act of 1903, after a strike on the Canadian Pacific Railroad. Again, the emphasis was on conciliation, but, if both sides agreed, arbitration could be had. However, the recommendations of the arbitrator were not binding, and no restraint was placed on strikes or lockouts. In 1906 a Conciliation and Labor Act was passed, but was inadequate and never used effectively.

The first major union legislation came in 1907, with the Industrial Disputes and Investigation Act, which was passed after a major coal mining strike. It brought under federal government intervention disputes in mining, transporation, communications, and public utilities. It established two principles that are also reflected one way or another in the legislation enacted by the provinces:

1. Compulsory conciliation.
2. Suspension of the right to strike or lockout until after the conciliation procedure has been completed and a waiting period has elapsed.

During World War I the IDI was extended to industries producing military supplies.

In 1925 a court decision stated that the act was outside the powers of the Parliament of Canada, that it infringed upon the exclusive authority of the provinces to legislate on matters involving property and civil rights. The act was then amended to apply to any dispute in conjunction with undertakings that were in the legislative jurisdiction of the Parliament. A clause in the act provided that any province could, if it wished, pass legislation voluntarily applying the federal policy to industry under provincial jurisdiction. Between 1925 and 1932 all provinces, except Prince Edward Island, did so. Later, Alberta and British Columbia passed their own laws.

In 1934 Quebec passed the Collective Labor Agreements Extension Act. It did not replace the existing coverage under the IDI, but laid the framework for a system of industrial relations combining collective bargaining with regulation. Other provinces passed comparable laws either as replacements for or supplements to the IDI as it applied in the provinces.

Although the provinces might have similar legislation, no uniform policy applied throughout Canada. Only the advent of World War II brought some uniformity, as the War Measures Act of 1939 saw all basic industries under the jurisdiction of federal policy. However, neither the IDI nor wartime measures dealt with important areas such as freedom of association, the right to negotiate, or recognition of a labor organization by an employer. During the war stronger legislation began to appear. Ontario enacted a Collective Bargaining Act in 1943 which went beyond the pre-war statutes of other provinces by actually setting up administrative and enforcement machinery. Passage of the act brought Ontario policy closer to that of the United States, although industrial relations in the province were still subject to the IDI Act as extended during the war. In 1944, however, Canada suspended the IDI; Privy Council Order 1003 introduced new control regulations which combined some principles of America's National Labor Relations Act with those of the IDI Act.

Privy Council Order 1003 superceded provincial legislation only during the war emergency. Among its provisions were: guarantee of labor's right to organize, selection of the appropriate unit for collective bargaining, certification of the bargaining agent, compulsory collective bargaining, and labor relations boards to investigate, and correct unfair labor practices. In disputes, conciliation was compulsory and strikes or lockouts were restrained. At the first stages of disputes, conciliation officers were to intervene. Conciliation boards were tripartite. Moreover, disputes that had not been settled when the agreement ws in effect had to be arbitrated.

Privy Council Order 1003 provided the basic for post-war industrial relations. In 1948 a new statute was enacted—the Industrial Relations and Disputes Investigation Act of 1948. Its jurisdiction (that of the federal government) was more restricted than the wartime emergency orders. The provinces, therefore, passed their own acts. Thus a variety of different laws govern about ninety-five percent of the work force.

In the succeeding years, provinces amended their laws or passed new statutes. In 1967 Canada passed the Public Services Staff Relations Act. Under this statute, organizations of federal government employees can negotiate agreements and can choose either binding arbitration of disputes without the right to strike or retain the right to strike and follow prescribed conciliation procedures. In most provinical jurisdictions separate legislation covers government and parapublic workers such as firefighters and teachers. The specific provisions differ in the various jurisdictions. The Canada Labor Code was enacted by the revised Statutes of Canada in 1970 and became effective in 1971. Among other laws it replaces the IDI. It continued the principle of postponing strikes and lockouts and set up machinery for conciliation of disputes. The code was amended by Statutes of Canada (1977–1978).

Basically, what is significant about labor relations in Canada is the greater extent of government intervention in labor disputes, compulsory conciliation and arbitration, the delay of strikes or lockouts while the proceedings are going on, and, in direct contrast to the United States, the greater power of provincial governments compared with the federal government. Critics say that compulsory conciliation and arbitration either circumvent or distort the collective bargaining concept and that delays in strikes may act more as a hotting up period than a cooling off period. Canada in recent years has had a high incidence of strikes, greater than that of comparable countries but less than that of the United States.

Canadian jurisdictions have legislation on collective bargaining. All employees have freedom of association and the right to choose a labor organization to represent them. Certification procedures exist for recognition of a union as exclusive bargaining agent. A certified union may compel an employer to bargain with it so as to reach an agreement. Unfair labor practices are prohibited. Government conciliation services are available to help the parties reach agreement; in some instances, conciliation is compulsory and strikes and lockouts are barred while the proceedings are in progress. Disputes arising while a contract is in effect must be resolved without work stoppages through the grievance procedure or, if necessary, by binding arbitration.

Most Canadian labor unions are affiliated with American international unions. The stresses and strains that have occurred seem to have become noticeably greater in recent years as Canadian nationalism has grown. Among the criticisms that have been made are domination by Americans, payment of large sums of money to the American international without receiving much in return and the insensitivity of American executives of internationals to the wishes of Canadian members.

American international unions have made their strong presence known in Canada. Stuart Jamieson cites the reasons why:

1. Competition: American unions might have feared competition from workers paid a lower wage. This may have been true earlier, but not any longer.

2. Profit for the unions: American unions might have sought more dues-paying members so that their revenues would have increased. Actually, most American unions had to subsidize their first organizing efforts in Canada. However, data now indicates that the dues paid the American unions have exceeded their expenditures. Some unions permit their Canadian branches to keep funds from per capita dues in balances to their own accounts in the United States rather than sending them to the American headquarters of the union.

3. Union growth: Like other large organizations, including corporations, unions are dominated by the need to survive and grow. Canada seems the logical place for expansion. Some unions, like some corporations, see Canadians as another kind of American and view Canada as the 51st state.

Apparently the main motivation comes from the Canadians themselves. By joining the American internationals the Canadians have been able to enjoy economic gains greater than they would have gotten on their own, especially when working for companies that are subsidiaries of large American multinational corporations.

In recent years challenges and criticism of Canadian links with American unions have increased in number and volume. The Chrysler local in Canada, for example, has not followed the lead of the American international, struck against the car manufacturer, and succeeded.

The Canadian Labor Congress at its 1970 convention prescribed minimum standards for American-affiliated unions:

1. Election of top Canadian officers by Canadians.

2. Granting decision-making authority in Canadian affairs to the Canadian officers.

3. Providing services appropriate to Canadian conditions.

The relations of most Canadian locals and district councils to their American internationals are about the same as those of American locals and councils. The chief Canadian officer is the equivalent of a regional or district vice president. The locals are represented at international onventions in the same ways as American locals. Theoretically, they are subject to the same rules and regulations under the union constitution.

In practice the actual control exerted over the Canadian locals varies from union to union. The nation has its own labor congress, its own labor laws. Unions other than American affiliates are represented in the congress. The degree of autonomy enjoyed by the American-affiliated unions depends on a number of variables. For instance:

1. The formal structure of the international, the constituion, the powers and prerogatives of the president and executive board, the methods of electing or appointing officers at all levels in the union hierarchy.

2. Informal and personal relationships at different executive levels, degrees of factionalism or unity, hostility or friendship, opposition or support.

3. Structure of the industry or trade.

The Canadian unions do enjoy almost complete autonomy in strikes. American union officials rarely call a Canadian strike— and they rarely exercise their veto power over strikes by Canadian locals or withhold strike funds.

The entire relationship between American internationals and their Canadian affiliates is at present in a state of flux. It is impossible to generalize or foresee the future other than to recognize that existing tension and the Canadian pressure for more autonomy must bring some changes.

The labor movements in the United States and Canada are similar to a marked degree. This is not surprising in view of our common heritage and our common language. In both nations labor organizations are free associations of free men in a free society within a framework of laws designed to encourage and to protect basic rights.

Glossary*

AGENCY SHOP: A union security clause whereby all members of a bargaining unit must pay a service fee, the equivalent of dues, whether or not they are union members.

AMERICAN PLAN: A post-World War I employer movement which stressed freedom of industry to manage its business without union interference.

APPRENTICE: An individual in training for a skilled trade.

ARBITRATION: The referral of collective bargaining or grievance disputes to an impartial third party. Usually the arbitrator's decision is final and binding, although there is advisory arbitration in which the decision of the arbitrator is taken under advisement by the parties.

AUTOMATION: Self-correcting feedback and computer electronics. Also, dramatic technological innovation of any sort at the workplace. Often regarded by unions as a cause of unemployment, job alienation, and dislocation.

*Definitions given are derived from those compiled by the United States Department of Labor and published in *The American Worker,* 1976.

BARGAINING UNIT: A specified group of employees empowered to bargain collectively with their employer.

BLUE-COLLAR WORKERS: Those in private and public employment who engage in manual labor or the skilled trades.

BOYCOTT: The term originated in 1880 when an Irish landowner, Captain Charles Boycott, was denied all services. Today the expression means collective pressure on employers by refusal to buy their goods or services.

BREAD-AND-BUTTER UNIONISM: Also called business unionism or pure-and-simple unionism. Adolph Strasser, president of the Cigar Makers Union and one of the founders of the AFL, once told a Congressional Committee: ''We have no ultimate ends. We are going from day to day. We fight only for immediate objectives —objectives that will be realized in a few years—we are all practical men.''

CENTRAL LABOR COUNCIL: A city or county federation of local unions which are affiliated with different national or international unions.

CHECKOFF: A clause in union contract authorizing the employer to deduct dues or service fees from employees' paychecks and remit them to the union.

CLOSED SHOP: The hiring and employment of union members only. Illegal under the Taft-Hartley Act.

COLLECTIVE BARGAINING: The determination of wages and other conditions of employment by direct negotiations between the union and employer.

COMPANY STORE: A store operated by a company for its employees. Often prices were higher here than elsewhere. Occasionally, workers were paid in script redeemable only at the company store.

COMPANY UNION: An employee association organized, controlled, and financed by the employer. Outlawed by the National Labor Relations Act.

CONCILIATION: An attempt by an impartial third party to reconcile differences between labor and management.

CONSPIRACY CASES: The Philadelphia cordwainers' case in 1806 and subsequent decisions involving labor disputes declared unions to be unlawful conspiracies. In 1842 the court decision in *Commonwealth* v. *Hunt* said that under certain circumstances unions were lawful.

CONSULTATION: Clauses in union contracts or in some state laws applicable to public employees stating that management must consult the union before making any major personnel changes.

CONTRACT LABOR: Workers signed a contract in Colonial times making them indentured servants for the life of the agreement. The system was later used to import Orientals into California and Hawaii and Italians and Greeks for work on the East Coast. It was bitterly fought by organized labor for the contract worker meant low wage competition.

COST-OF-LIVING INDEX: The Consumer Price Index prepared by the United States Bureau of Labor Statistics. The Index measures changes in the cost of living month by month, year by year.

CRAFT UNIONS: Trade unions organized along lines of their skilled crafts. They formed the base of the American Federation of Labor.

CRIMINAL SYNDICALISM: Syndicalism comes from the French word for union, *syndicat*. Syndicalists believe unions should run the economy. The term is associated with the Industrial Workers of the World. Half the states just after World War I passed criminal syndicalist laws. In California a person could be convicted for having once belonged to the IWW. In New Mexico, an employer could be prosecuted for hiring an alleged anarchist.

DISCRIMINATION: Unequal treatment of workers because of race, sex, religion, nationality, or union membership.

DUAL-UNIONISM: The AFL expelled most CIO unions in 1937 for dual unionism because industrial unions were encroaching on the jurisdiction of craft unions within factories.

ESCALATOR CLAUSE: A clause in the union contract which

provides for a cost-of-living increase in wages by relating wages to changes in consumer prices. Usually the Consumer Price Index is used as the measure of price changes.

FAIR LABOR STANDARDS ACT: Passed in 1938, this law set minimum wages and overtime rates and prohibited child labor for industry connected with interstate commerce.

FALL RIVER SYSTEM: The factory system which employed men, women, and children and made no special provisions for their housing.

FEATHERBEDDING: Employing more workers than are actually necessary to complete a task.

FREE RIDER: A worker in the bargaining unit who refuses to join the union but accepts all the benefits negotiated by the union. Also called a freeloader.

FRINGE BENEFITS: Negotiated gains other than wages such as vacations, holidays, pensions, insurance, and supplemental unemployment benefits.

GAG ORDER: President Theodore Roosevelt issued an executive order dubbed by unions the gag order which forbade federal employees on pain of dismissal to seek legislation on their behalf except through their own department.

GOON: A person brought in from the outside to break strikes and union-organizing attempts.

GOVERNMENT BY INJUNCTION: The use of the injunction by government to break strikes.

GREENBACKISM: Reference to partisans of the Greenback Party and the Greenback Labor Party of the 1870s. Greenbackers advocated increased issues of paper money to make cash more readily available to people. They also demanded shorter work hours, abolition of convict labor, boards of labor statistics, and restrictions on immigrant labor.

GRIEVANCE COMMITTEE: A committee within the local union which processes grievances arising from the violation of the contract, state or federal law, or an abuse of a shop's past practice.

HOT CARGO: A clause in a union contract which says that workers cannot be compelled to handle goods from an employer involved in a strike.

IMPROVEMENT FACTOR: An annual wage increase negotiated by the union and management which recognizes that the rising productivity of workers contributes to the company's profitability.

INCENTIVE PAY: A system based on the amount of production turned out by workers.

INDENTURED SERVANT: A person bound through a contract to the service of another person for a specified amount of time.

INDUSTRIAL DEMOCRACY: A phrase once used to describe unions as a humanizing force at the workplace. In the 1970s and 1980s it means worker participation in management decision-making.

INDUSTRIAL REVOLUTION: The great advances in technology beginning in the late eighteenth century turned America from a handicraft economy into one of technological mass production.

INDUSTRIAL UNION: A union which includes all the workers in an industry regardless of their craft. Industrial unions formed the base of the CIO.

INJUCTION: A court order which prohibits a party from taking a particular course of action, such as picketing in the case of a union on strike.

INTERNATIONAL UNION: A union with members in both the United States and Canada.

JOURNEYMAN: A worker who has completed his apprenticeship in a trade or craft and is therefore considered a qualified, skilled worker.

JURISDICTIONAL DISPUTES: Arguments among unions over which union represents workers at a job site.

LANDRUM-GRIFFIN ACT: The Labor-Management Reporting and Disclosure Act of 1959. The law contains regulations for union election procedures and supervision of their financial affairs by the United States Department of Labor.

LITTLE STEEL FORMULA: The World War II War Labor Board introduced this formula which tied the cost of living to wage increases as a stabilization factor.

LOCKOUT: When an employer closes down the factory in order to coerce workers into meeting his demands or modifying their demands.

LOWELL SYSTEM: The system associated with Lowell, Massachusetts, whereby workers, mainly young women, lived in boardinghouses owned and run by the company.

MAINTENANCE OF MEMBERSHIP: A provision in the union contract which says that a worker who voluntarily joins the union must remain a member for the duration of the agreement.

MASSACRE: Union descriptions of tragic events in labor history. Examples include Chicago's Memorial Day Massacre where ten steelworkers were shot dead and over eighty were wounded by police on May 30, 1937. There was the Hilo, Hawaii, Massacre of 1938 where nearly fifty unionists were shot or bayonetted by police while sitting on a government pier protesting the unloading of a struck ship.

MEDIATION: Attempts by an impartial third party to get labor and management to find agreement during a dispute.

MERIT SYSTEM: The major grievance of public employees was the indignity and insecurity fostered by the political patronage system which ruled government employment. They wanted a system where they would be hired and promoted on their merit. The merit system was introduced by passage of the Civil Service Act of 1883.

MINIMUM WAGE: The lowest rate of pay an employer is allowed to pay under the law or a union contract.

MODIFIED UNION SHOP: A provision in the union contract requiring all new employees to join the union and requiring all workers already in the union to remain as union members.

MOHAWK VALLEY FORMULA: Developed by James Rand, president of Remington Rand, in 1936 to break strikes. The formula included discrediting union leaders by calling them "agitators," threatening to move the plant, raising the banner of law and order to mobilize the community against the union, and actively engaging police in strike-breaking activity, then organizing a back-to-work movement of pro-company employees. While the National Association of Manufacturers enthusiastically published the plan, the National Labor Relations Board called it a battle plan for industrial war.

MOLLY MAGUIRES: A group of Irish miners who, in the 1860s and '70s, vandalized the mines and terrorized the bosses. Ten were hanged as the leaders of the conspiracy after Pinkerton agent James McParland exposed them in 1877.

MOONLIGHTING: Working more than one job.

NATIONAL LABOR RELATIONS ACT OF 1935: Also known as the Wagner Act after the law's chief sponsor, Senator Robert Wagner of New York. It represented a fundamental turnaround in government's attitudes toward labor relations. The law created a National Labor Relations Board to carry out its goals of guaranteeing the right of workers to form unions of their own choosing and to bargain collectively with employers.

ONE BIG UNION: The slogan of the IWW which stressed inclusion of everyone, regardless of trade, into an all-encompassing union. This was also the rationale for the general strike where workers in all type of employment would strike at the same time.

OPEN SHOP: A business that employs workers without regard to union membership. In the 1920s the open shop was an ill-disguised attempt to get rid of bona fide unions. States with right to work laws have decreed the open shop.

PACE-SETTER: A method of speeding up work. The pace-setter is a person who sets the work pace, usually at an even higher rate, by leading the work gang and necessitating its catching up with him.

PALMER RAIDS: In 1919-20, United States Attorney General A. Mitchell Palmer conducted raids on the headquarters of alleged radicals. Unionists, liberals, radicals, and aliens were indiscriminately arrested. About four hundred were tried for their dissent from the status quo with little regard for their civil rights.

PATERNALISM: The company that considered itself the father of its employees and as such had the responsibility of regulating their lives through company houses, stores, hospitals, theaters, sports programs, churches, publications, and codes of behavior on and off the job. Paternalism was also prevalent in public employment. In 1915 teachers were not permitted to marry, keep company with men, travel beyond the city limits, smoke, dress in bright colors, or wear skirts shorter than two inches above the ankles.

PERB: The abbreviation of state public employment relations boards.

PICKETING: The stationing of persons outside a place of employment to publically protest the employer and to discourage entry of nonstriking workers or customers. Most picketing takes place during strikes although there is also informational picketing conducted against nonunion business establishments.

PIECEWORK: The incentive wage system by which workers are paid by the individual piece worked on or completed.

PINKERTONS: Agents of the Allan Pinkerton Detective Agency of Chicago who were hired by employers to break strikes or act as company spies within unions. Some believe the expression "fink," a pejorative term for a worker not loyal to the union, originated by combining a common expletive with the word Pinkerton.

POLITICAL ACTION: Unions engaged in political action at least as far back as the 1820s, when they demanded universal free public education and abolition of imprisonment for debt as their major social reform issues. Today, AFL-CIO and independent unions expend a substantial amount of money and effort in the promotion of their political causes. Their rationale is that what is gained at the bargaining table can be taken away from unions through legislation. AFL-CIO's formal political organization which functions at the national, state, community and local union level is the Committee on Political Education (COPE).

PREVAILING WAGE: In 1861, Congress passed a prevailing wage rate law which said in part: ''That the hours of labor and the rates of wages of the employees in the navy yards shall conform as nearly as possible with those of private establishments in the immediate vicinity of the respective yards.''

PRODUCTIVITY: The measure of efficiency in production. The comparison of resources used in creating goods and services. If the same resources that were used in the past produce more goods and services, productivity has increased.

PROHIBITED PRACTICES: Generally used in public employment to describe unfair labor practices on the part of employer and employee organizations.

READING FORMULA: The procedure with which union recognition was achieved in factories during the 1930s. Rather than being compelled to strike for union recognition, the new Wagner Act provided a method of union representation elections which were conducted by the National Labor Relations Board.

REAL WAGES: Wages expressed in terms of what today's dollar will buy. A common method of determining buying power is through the Consumer Price Index.

REDEMPTIONER: A white emigrant from Europe who paid for his or her voyage to the New World by acting as a servant for a specific period of time. Also knows as a freewiller.

RIGHT TO WORK LAWS: The term used by opponents of unions to institute open shop laws in the state. The expression has nothing to do with guaranteeing anyone the right to a job.

SABOTAGE: From the French word *sabot* or wooden shoe which workers threw into the machines to keep them from working. Workers have been perpetually fearful that new machines would take their jobs away from them and sabotage was one of their early answers to the Industrial Revolution. It was also a part of strike violence where strikes incapacitated machines or buildings in order to shut down production.

SCAB: A worker who refuses to join the union or who works while others are striking. Also knows as a strikebreaker.

SECONDARY BOYCOTT: An effort to disrupt the business of an employer through boycott techniques, even though his own workers are not directly involved in the labor dispute.

SENIORITY: A worker's length of service with an employer. In union contracts, seniority often determines layoffs from work, and recalls back to work.

SEPARATION PAY: Payment to a worker who is permanently laid off his job through no fault of his own.

SERVICE FEE: Money, usually the equivalent of union dues, which members of an agency shop bargaining unit pay the union for negotiating and administerating the collective bargaining agreement.

SIT-DOWN STRIKE: In June, 1934, Rex Murray, president of the General Tire local in Akron, Ohio, discussed a pending strike with fellow unionists. If they used bricks, the police would beat them up. But if they sat down inside the plant and hugged the machines, the police wouldn't use violence. They might hurt the machines: So began the era of the sit-down strikes effectively used by unions like the Rubber Workers and Auto Workers to build the CIO. The sit-down period lasted only through 1937, but it provided labor history with one of its most colorful chapters.

SLOWDOWN: A form of protest where workers deliberately lessen the amount of work for a particular purpose.

SOCIAL UNIONISM: Unions which look beyond immediate objectives to try to reform social conditions and which also consider unionsim as a means of appealing to needs of members which are not strictly economic. In addition to fighting for economic gains, social unions have education, health, welfare, artistic, recreation, and citizenship programs to attempt to satisfy needs of members. Labor, social unionists believe, has an obligation to better the general society.

SPEED UP: A word used by workers to describe employer attempts to increase their output without increasing their wages.

STATE SOVEREIGNTY: The idea that the state is king and public employees had no right to make demands on it. In 1949 a New York court said: "To tolerate or recognize any combination of civil service employees of the government as a labor organization or union is not only incompatible with the spirit of democracy but inconsistent with every principle upon which our government is founded."

STOOLPIGEON: A person hired by an employer to infiltrate the union and report on its activities.

STRETCHOUT: A workload increase that does not grant a commensurate pay increase.

STRIKE: A temporary work stoppage by workers to support their demands on an employer. Also called a turn out early in the nineteenth century.

SUBCONTRACTING: The practice of employers getting work done by an outside contractor and not by workers in the bargaining unit. Also called contracting out.

SUPPLEMENTAL UNEMPLOYMENT BENEFITS: A provision in the union contract which provided laid-off workers with benefits in addition to unemployment compensation.

SYMPATHY STRIKE: A strike by persons not directly involved in a labor dispute in order to show solidarity with the original strikers and increase pressure on the employer.

TAFT-HARTLEY ACT: In 1947, Congress passed this act which outlawed the closed shop, jurisdictional strikes, and secondary boycotts. It set up machinery for decertifying unions and allowed the states to pass more stringent legislation against unions such as right-to-work laws. Employers and unions were forbidden to contribute funds out of their treasuries to candidates for federal office, supervision was denied union protection, and the unions seeking the services of the National Labor Relations Board had to file their constitutions, by-laws, and financial statements with United States Department of Labor. Their officers also had to sign a non-communist affidavit.

TAYLORISM: Associated with the principles of scientific management advocated by Frederick W. Taylor at the beginning of the twentieth century. Taylor proposed time and motion studies of jobs to enable managers to set standards for more efficient production.

UNFAIR LABOR PRACTICES: Defined by the National Labor Relations Act and by the Taft-Hartley Act as practices of discrimination, coercion, and intimidation prohibited to labor and management. Management cannot form company unions or use coercive tactics to discourage union organization. Unions cannot force workers to join organizations not of their own choosing.

UNION LABEL: A stamp or tag on products to show that the work was done by union labor.

UNION SECURITY: A clause in the contract providing for the union shop, maintenance of membership, or the agency shop.

UNION SHOP: A shop where every member of the bargaining unit must become a member of the union after a specified amount of time.

WALKING DELEGATE: A unionist who policed jobs to see that workers were getting fair treatment.

WHITE-COLLAR WORKERS: Workers who have office jobs rather than factory, farm, or construction work.

WOBBLIES: A nickname for members of the Industrial Workers of the World. The origin of the word is unknown.

YELLOW-DOG CONTRACT: A contract a worker was compelled to sign stating that he or she would not join a union. The practice was outlawed in 1932 by the passage of the Norris-La-Guardia Act.

Suggestions for Further Reading

American Worker, The. U.S. Department of Labor. Washington, D.C., 1976.

Bakke, E. Wight. *Mutual Survival: The Goal of Unions and Management*, 2nd edition. Hamden, CT: Archon, 1966.

Barbash, Jack. *American Unions: Government, Structure and Politics*. New York: Random House, 1967.

————*Labor's Grass Roots*. New York: Harper & Brothers, 1961.

Beal, Edwin F., Edward D. Wickersham and Philip K. Kienast. *The Practice of Collective Bargaining*, 5th edition. Homewood, Ill.: Richard D. Irwin, Inc., 1976.

Bernstein, Irving. *Turbulent Years*. Boston: Houghton-Mifflin, 1970.

Blackburn, Jack and G. Busman. *Understanding Unions in the Public Sector*. Los Angeles: Institute of Industrial Relations, University of California, 1977.

Bok, Derek C. and John T. Dunlop. *Labor and the American Community*. New York: Simon and Schuster, 1970.

Brill, Stephen. *The Teamsters*. New York: Simon and Schuster, 1978.

Brooks, Thomas R.. *Toil and Trouble*, 2nd edition. New York: Dell Publishing Co., Inc., 1971.

Chamberlain, Neil W.. *Labor*. New York: McGraw-Hill Book Company, Inc., 1958.

Cohen, Sanford. *Labor in the United States*. Columbus, Ohio: Charles E. Merrill Books, Inc., 1979.

Cox, Archibald. *Law and the National Labor Policy*. Los Angeles: University of California Press, 1960.

Crispo, John. *International Unionism—A Study in Canadian-American Relations*. Toronto: McGraw-Hill Book Company, Inc., 1962.

Davey, Harold W.. *Contemporary Collective Bargaining*, 3rd edition. Englewood Cliffs, N.J.: Prentice-Hall, Inc., 1972.

French, Doris. *Faith, Sweat and Politics, The Early Trade Union Years in Canada*. Toronto: McClelland & Stewart, 1962.

Jamieson, Stuart. *Industrial Relations in Canada*, 2nd edition. Toronto: Macmillan of Canada, 1963.

Labour Relations Legislation in Canada. Legislative Branch, Canada Department of Labour. Ottowa: 1970.

Levine, Louis. *The Women's Garment Workers, A History of the ILGWU*. New York: B.V. Huebsch, 1924.

Meier, August and Elliot Rudwick. *Black Detroit and the Rise of the UAW*. New York: Oxford University Press, 1979.

Mills, Daniel Quinn. *Labor-Management Relations*, 2nd edition. New York: McGraw-Hill Book Company Inc., 1982.

Morris, Richard B.. *Government and Labor in Early America*. New York: Columbia University Press, 1946.

Pelling, Henry. *American Labor*. Chicago: The University of Chicago Press, 1960.

Perlman, Selig and Philip Taft. *History of Labor in the United States, 1896–1932*. New York: Macmillan, 1935.

Peterson, Florence. *American Labor Unions*, revised edition. New York: Harper & Brothers, 1952.

Purcell, Theodore V.. *Blue-Collar Man: Patterns of Dual Al-*

legiance in Industry. Cambridge, Mass.: Harvard University Press, 1960.

Robinson, Archie. *George Meany and His Times*. New York: Simon and Schuster, 1981.

Sayles, Leonard R. and George Strauss. *The Local Union*. New York: Harper & Brothers, 1953.

Stolberg, Benjamin. *The Story of the CIO*. New York: Arno Press, 1938.

Stone, Morris. *Labor-Management Contracts at Work*. New York: Harper & Brothers, 1961.

Taft, Philip. *Organized Labor in American History*. New York: Harper & Brothers, 1964.

————*Corruption qnd Racketeering in the Labor Movement*. Ithica, N.Y.: Cornell University Press, 1970.

Taylor, Benjamin J. and Fred Whitney. *Labor Relations Law*, 3rd edition. Englewood Cliffs, N.J.: Prentice-Hall, Inc., 1979.

Woods, H.D. and Sylvia Ostrey. *Labour Policy and Labour Economics in Canada*. Toronto: Macmillan of Canada, 1962.

Index

Across-the-board increase, 161
Adamson Act, 62, 63
Agency shop, 186
Air Traffic Controllers strike, 109, 181
All-Canadian Congress of Labor (ACCL), 195, 196
Amalgamated Association of Iron and Steel Workers strike, 46, 47
Amalgamated local, 118
American Anti-Boycott Association, 54, 186
American Arbitration Association, 186
American Federation of Labor, 28:
  bias to and craft unionism, 114
  conflict over industrial unionism, 81, 82
  Craft union organization, 67
  Danbury Hatters case, 58
  effect on Canadian unions, 194
  establishment, 39
  growth at end of 19th century, 43
  membership, 61
  no-discrimination policy, 101, 102
American Federation of Labor and Congress of Industrial Organizations:
  direct charter of local union, 114
  executive council, 123, 124
  merger, 93, 94
  number of affiliates, 125
  officers, 123
  resolution of jurisdictional disputes, 126, 127
  trade and industrial departments, 124
American Labor Union, 59
"American Plan," 66
American Railway Union, 47, 48
Anti-union practices, 57, 66, 67, 83, 84, 97
Arbitration, 111, 172, 184–189, 202, 203
Arbitrator, 186–187

Back-to-work movement, 181, 182
Barbash, Jack, 29, 95
Bargaining unit, 155
Bernstein, Irving, 83

Black workers, 97–100
  and National Labor Union, 28
  sanitation, strike by, 106
  slave labor, 17, 18
Blacklist, 29, 50, 54, 55, 57
Boston police strike, 64
Bound labor, 16
Boycott, 29, 36, 48, 56, 92
Bridge and Structural Workers, Intl. Association of: 50, 51
Brooks, Thomas R., 20, 31, 33, 46, 47, 65, 66, 67
Brotherhood of Locomotive Engineers, 28, 32

Brotherhood of Locomotive Firemen and
    Engineers, 47, 96
Brotherhood of Maintenance of Way Em-
    ployees, 47
Brotherhood of Railway Clerks, 70
Brotherhood of Railroad Trainmen, 47
Brotherhood of Sleeping Car Porters, 100
Building trades, 103, 129, 155
Bureau of Labor Statistics, 161
Business agent, 116

Call-in-pay and Call-back pay, 163
Canada, 200–203:
    and development of industry in, 191
    labor legislation, 199
    majority rule principle, 170
    population differences, 191
    public policy on collective bargaining,
        169
Canadian Brotherhood of Railroad
    Employees (CBRE), 195
Canadian Congress of Labor (CCL), 196
Canadian Federation of Labor, 195
Canadian Labor Congress (CLC), 197
Canadian Labor Union, 193
Canadian Seamen's Union, 196, 197
"Captive" mines, organization of, 75, 76
Carey, James, 82
Chamberlain, Neil, 80, 81
Checkoff, 156
Child labor, 44, 45
Citizens Industrial Association, 54, 55
Civil conspiracy doctrine, 22
Civil Rights Act of 1964, 102, 103, 105,
    136
Clayton Act, 58, 62, 68
Cleveland, Grover, 45, 49
Closed shop, 22, 92, 129, 155
Cohen, Sanford, 31, 33, 37, 56, 57, 74
Collective bargaining, 167–173:
    by supervisors or managers, 141
    employers' obligation, 132, 164
    federal government and, 107, 111, 112
    for social benefits, 50
    government employees and, 107, 112
    grievance processing, 146, 147
    in Canada, 201, 203
    international union and, 120
    local union and, 115
    under National Labor Relations Act, 75
    wage provisions, 160, 161
Colonial era, 15, 19, 21
Committee for Industrial Organizations, 82
Commonwealth vs. Hunt, 22
Communists:
    in Canadian labor movement, 195, 196

in ILGWU, 68
purged from CIO, 93, 95
Company town, 47, 48
Company union, 50, 63, 66, 70, 78
Consumer Price Index, 161, 162
Conciliation Act, 200
Conciliation, compulsory in Canada, 200,
    203
Conciliator, 186
Confederation des Travailleurs Catholiques
    du Canada (CTCC), 197, 199
Congress of Industrial Organizations: See
    also American Federation of Labor
    and Congress of Industrial
    Organizations
    effect on Canadian labor, 195, 196
    establishment, 82
    organization of black workers, 97, 101
Contract, union, 155–161:
    arbitration provision, 186
    health and welfare provisions, 165, 166
    interpretation through grievance
        procedure, 185
    pension provisions, 166
    ratification, 174
    violations, 146
Coolidge, Calvin, 64
Coronado Coal cases, 58
Courts and labor unions, 55
Craft union, 23, 113, 136, 137
Criminal conspiracy, 21, 22, 200

Danbury Hatters, 43, 58
Debs, Eugene V., 47, 48
Discharge/Discipline, 130, 131, 158–159
Discrimination, 78, 103, 105, 136, 159
Dominion Trades and Labor Congress, 194
District trade council, 118
Dubinsky, David, 82
Dues and assessments, union, 126
Duplex vs. Deering, 68

Economic Stabilization Act during World
    War II, 89
Eight-hour day, 28, 38, 62, 63
Emigration: See Immigration
Employee Retirement Income Security Act
    of 1974, 166
Employees, non-union, 158, 161, 162
Employer, 54, 58, 66, 78, 171, 181, 182
Employer-union cooperation, 149, 166
Equal Employment Opportunity Act, 136
Erdman Act, 56, 68
Exclusive representation, 155
Executive Orders, 110-111

Fair Labor Standards Act of 1938, 162
Federal Labor Relations Council, 111
Federal Mediation and Conciliation
    Service, 92, 159, 172, 186
Federation of Organized Trades and Labor
    Unions of the United States and
    Canada, 38
Federal Service Impasse Council, 111
Federal troops, 32, 45, 48, 53
Fines, union, 126
Ford, Henry, 86
Ford Motor Company, 96
Fraser, Douglas, 174
Freewillers, 16
French:
    labor movement in Canada, 197
    settlers in Canada, 190
Fringe benefits, 89, 165

General wage increase, 161
Government:
    Canadian, policy toward labor, 199
    federal system in Canada, 192
    policy on collective bargaining, 169, 170
Government employees:
    as union members, 11
    civil service associations, 97
    Executive orders 10988 and 11491, 107,
        111
    legislation in Canada, 202
    New York City, 107
    state, 107
Great Depression, 49
Green, William, 67, 93
Grievance procedure:
    as major union function, 146, 147
    description, 184, 185
    discharge and, 130
    in federal service, 111
    role of union steward, 117
    under union contract, 158, 159
Guaranteed annual wage, 96

Haymarket Square explosion, 38, 39
Hayward, Big Bill, 60
Health and safety, 147–149
Health and welfare under union contract,
    166
Hillman, Sidney, 82
Hispanic workers, 99, 107
Holidays and holiday pay, 164
Hoover, Herbert, 71, 73, 74
Hughes, Charles Evans, 71, 79

Immigrants, 24, 97, 152, 193
Immigration, 15, 16, 27, 45, 67
Indentured servants, 16, 19

Industrial Disputes and Investigation Act of
    1907, 200, 201
Industrial Relations and Disputes Act of
    1948, 202
Industrial union definition, 114
Industrial Workers of the World, 43, 59,
    60, 63, 64, 194
Industry:
    automobile, organization in, 85, 86
    development in Canada, 191
    growth in 19th century, 42
    organization by CIO, 83
Initiation fees, union, 125
Injunctions, labor:
    as anti-union weapon, 29, 54, 56
    explanation of, 69
    in Pullman strike, 48
    use in 19th century, 22
    Norris-LaGuardia Act and, 70
Internal Disputes Plan, 126
International Association of Machinists,
    67, 101, 112
International Industrial Assembly of North
    America, 28
International Ladies Garment Workers
    Union, 49, 68, 97, 105, 148, 150,
    151, 152, 165
International union, 115, 119–122:
    approval of strike by, 178
    relationship with Canadian unions, 203,
    205
Iron Molders' Union, 23, 25
Iron, Steel and Tin Workers, 50

Jamieson, Stuart, 191, 192, 199
Job security, 96, 131
Johnson, Lyndon, 103
Joint board, 118
Journeymen Cordwainers of Philadelphia,
    21
Jurisdictional disputes, 92, 127

Kennedy, John F., 102, 103, 110
King, Martin Luther, 106
Knights of Labor, 34–39, 194
Knights of St. Erispin, 30

Labor agreement: See Contract, union
Labor-Management Relations Act: See
    Taft-Hartley Act.
Labor-Management Reporting and
    Disclosure Act of 1959: See
    Landrum-Griffin Act of 1959
Labor spies, 29, 54, 55, 67
Labor supply, in colonial era, 16, 18
LaFollette Seamen's Act, 62
Landrum-Griffin Act of 1959, 91, 94–95,

119, 121, 126, 138, 139, 155
Layoff, 130, 131, 157, 158
Lewis, John L., 75, 81, 82, 83, 84, 86, 87, 88, 89, 90, 91, 147
"Little Steel" Organization by SWOC, 84, 85
"Little Steel" Formula, 85
Local unions, 113–118, 178
Lockout, 159, 183
Ludlow Massacre, 52, 54, 62

Machinists and Blacksmiths' International Union, 25
Maintenance of membership, 92, 156, 157
Mass picketing, 180
Meany, George, 93, 94, 102
Mechanics' Union of Trade Associations, 23
Mediator, 186
Memorial Day Massacre, 84
Mines, seizure by U.S. during World War II, 90
Molders and Allied Workers' Union, 23
Molly Maguires, 29, 30
Montgomery, David, 34, 41, 42
Morris, Richard B., 15, 18
Murray, Philip, 82, 86, 93

National Defense Mediation Board, 87
National Federation of Independent Unions, 125
National Founders' Association, 54
National Guard: See State militia
National Industrial Recovery Act, 75, 76
National Labor Relations Act, 70, 75–79, 195
National Labor Relations Board, 77, 78, 92, 126, 155, 177
National Labor Union, 23, 28
National Metal Trades Association, 54, 55, 67
National Trades' Union, 24
National Typographical Union, 25
National union, See international union
National War Labor Board, 63, 88–89, 165
Negotiations: See Collective Bargaining
Nixon, Richard M., 111
Norris-LaGuardia Act of 1932, 23, 69, 71, 72, 169, 170
No-strike pledge, during World War I, 63
Nurses' unions, 111

Occupational Health and Safety Act of 1970, 149
One Big Union (OBU), 195, 196
Open shop, 50, 66

Organizing, 144, 145, 192
Oriental workers, 99
Overtime pay, 162, 163

Paternalism, 52, 66: See also Rockefeller Plan
Pelling, Henry, 44, 49
Pension plans, 166
Personal leave, 164
Pessen, Edward, 24, 25, 26
Peterson, Florence, 66
Picketing, 56, 179, 180
Pinkertons, 30, 38, 44, 46
Portal-to-portal pay, 90
Postal workers, 108, 109
Powderly, Terence V., 36, 38, 39
Premium pay, 162, 163
Professional employees, 37, 111, 112, 191
Professional sports' unions, 112
Promotions, 158
Public employees: See Government employees
Pullman strike, 45, 47, 48, 49
Public Services Staff Relations Act, 202

Racketeering in unions, 67–68, 93, 95
Railroad Riots, 30, 33
Railroads:
   black workers and, 100
   Brotherhoods in Canada, 193
   Eight-hour day, on, 62, 63
   Erdman Act, 56
   Railway Labor Act, 70, 71
   seizure during World War II, 89
Railway Labor Act of 1926, 70, 71
Railway Labor Board, 70
Railway Labor Disputes Act of 1903, 201
Randolph, A. Philip, 100, 101
Recession:
   after Civil War, 28
   of 1837, 24
   Panic of 1857, 25
   Panic of 1873, 30, 42
   1893 to 1897, 42
Redemptioners, 16
Reinstatement fee, 125, 139
Reuther, Walter, 82, 86, 93, 94
Right to strike by government employees, 109, 110
Right-to-work laws, 92, 129, 157
Roberts, Harold S., 113, 114, 127
Rockefeller, John D., 52, 54
Rockefeller Plan, 52: See also Paternalism
Roosevelt, Franklin D., 74, 86, 87, 88, 101, 110
Roosevelt, Theodore, 45, 49, 51, 52

Seniority, 131, 157, 158
Sherman Antitrust Act, 42, 44, 57, 58
Sick leave, paid, 164
Slave labor, 17
Socialist Trade and Labor Alliance, 59
Sloane, Arthur A., 19
Sons of Vulcan, 50
Spies, industrial: *See* Labor spies
State militia, 33, 46, 53, 64
Steel Workers Organizing Committee
    (SWOC), 47, 83, 84
Stephens, Uriah, 34, 36
Strike/Strikes:
    after World War I, 64
    and lockout, suspension in Canada, 200
    as criminal conspiracy, 21
    in 18th century, 24
    Boston police, 64
    by Federation of Organized Trades and
        Labor Unions, 38
    by Knights of Labor, 34, 37
    Canadian Broadcasting Company, 199
    economic, 177
    financial considerations, 179
    government employees and, 108, 110
    Homestead, 46, 47
    in 18th century, 19–21
    international union's role, 120
    jurisdictional, 92
    Lawrence, Massachusetts, 59
    legality of, 176, 177
    Memphis, Tennessee, sanitation
        workers, 106
    picketing during, 180
    prevention in Canada, 192
    printers in 18th century, 19, 20
    public relations during, 180, 181
    Pullman, 45
    railroad, 47, 49
    Republic Steel, 84
    sit-down, 83, 85
    unfair labor practice, 177
    union procedure, 178
    union steward's role, 117
    United States Steel Corporation, 50, 64,
        66
    upon contract termination, 159
Strikebreakers, 29, 38, 54, 55, 67, 183
Sweatshop, 148
"Sweetheart" contract, 172
Sylvis, William H., 23

Taft-Hartley Act of 1947, 91–93:
    closed shop and, 129, 155
    contract termination or modification
        under, 159
    exclusion of supervisors and managers,
        141
    illegal strikes under, 177
    professional employees and, 141
    jurisdictional disputes and, 126
    right-to-work laws and, 157
    union initiation fees and, 126
    union membership rules and, 135
Taft, Philip, 51, 54, 55, 74
Taylor Act, 108
Teachers' unions, 111
Teamsters, International Brotherhood of,
    113
Telecommunications International Union,
    125
Tompkins Square Riot, 31, 32
Toronto Trades and Labor Council, 194
Trades and Labor Congress of Canada
    (TLC), 194, 195
Trades assemblies, 26
Trades Union Act, 200
Trainmen's Union, 32
Triangle Shirtwaist Company fire, 44, 61,
    147, 148
Truman, Harry S., 91, 102
Trusts, 42, 57
Typographical Society, 20
Typographical Union, 23

Unemployment, 42, 73
Unfair labor practices, 77, 78, 92, 175,
    177, 203
Union/Unions:
    affiliated, 125
    apprentices, 136, 137
    black officers in, 104
    city central, 23
    Civil War, and, 26–28
    constitution and bylaws, 115, 119
    contract: *See* Contract, union
    crime and corruption in, 135
    demands in contract negotiations, 172,
        173
    district trade council, 118
    dues and fees, 126, 140
    during World War II, 86, 90
    educational activities, 151, 152
    18th century, 21
    expansion, 43, 80
    expenses, 125, 126
    expulsion of officers, 115
    finances, 119, 125, 126
    government employees and, 107
    health and safety activities, 147, 148,
        165–166
    in Canada during 19th century, 193

international or national, 118, 122
joint board, 118
leadership opportunities, 133
local: *See* Local Union
membership: *See* Union membership
mergers, 128
19th century, 23, 35
obligation to bargain, 175
organizing, 122, 144, 145
political activities, 149, 150
preparations for strike, 180, 181
segregated locals, 102
staff workers, 122
stewards, 116, 117, 146
strike fund, 179
support of Canadian strikes, 198
trusteeship, 119
unaffiliated, 125
women workers and, 104, 105, 106
Union membership:
    decline in 1920s, 67
    disciplinary rules, 139
    discriminatory bars, 99, 135, 136
    during layoff or leave, 140
    during World War II, 90
    expulsion from, 138
    provisions for, 135, 136
    reasons for joining, 129, 130, 132, 133
    reasons for refraining from, 134, 135
    regulations, 136, 138
    retirement or withdrawal from, 140, 141
    suspension and reinstatement, 139
    transfer, 140
    withdrawal from, 138
Union Security, 92, 129–130, 155–157:
    See also Right-to-work laws
Union Shop, 129, 130, 156
United Automobile Workers, 85
United Hatters Union, 58
United Mine Workers, 45, 51–54, 75–76,
    87–88, 96–97, 113, 147
United States:
    Conciliation Service, 62
    Department of Labor, establishment, 62
    government attitudes toward labor and
        unions, 45, 49, 71
    influence on Canadian labor relations,
        192

population, 19, 20, 27, 45
United States Steel Corporation, 50, 64,
    66, 83

Vacations and vacation pay, 164
Vertical union: *See* Industrial Union
Veterans' Bonus March, 74

Wages, 158, 160–163
Wage and Hour Act: *See* Fair Labor
    Standards Act
Wagner Act: *See* National Labor Relations
    Act
Western Federation of Miners, 59
Western Labor Congress, 195
Western Labor Union, 59
White collar workers, 97
Wilson, Woodrow, 49, 52, 53, 60
Wobblies, *See* Industrial Workers of the
    World
Work councils: *See* Company unions
Witney, Fred, 19
Women:
    and Knights of Labor, 34, 35
    and National Labor Union, 28
    discrimination against, 97
    union attitude toward, 104, 105
Women's Suffrage Association, 28
Workers:
    health and safety, 44, 45
    hospital, 11
    living conditions, 18, 41, 42
    minority, 97, 104—*See also* Black
        workers, Women
    postal, 12
    professional, 11, 12
    sanitation, 11
Workers' compensation, 44, 149
Working conditions in factories, 148
World War I, 59–63
World War II:
    ban on discrimination in defense
        industries, 102
    evolution on fringe benefits, 165
    labor policy in Canada, 201
    strike during, 87

Yellow dog contract, 29, 54, 56, 57, 68, 72